Joy Awaits

Joy Awaits

A Guide to Spiritual Paths of Peace, Love, and Healing

Dorothy Leeda Jones, PhD

Transpersonal Psychologist

BALBOA.
PRESS
A DIVISION OF HAY HOUSE

ISBN: 978-1-4525-5222-4 (sc)
ISBN: 978-1-4525-5223-1 (hc)
ISBN: 978-1-4525-5221-7 (e)

Library of Congress Control Number: 2012908677

Balboa Press books may be ordered through booksellers or by contacting:

Balboa Press
A Division of Hay House
1663 Liberty Drive
Bloomington, IN 47403
www.balboapress.com
1-(877) 407-4847

Because of the dynamic nature of the Internet, any web addresses or links contained in this book may have changed since publication and may no longer be valid. The views expressed in this work are solely those of the author and do not necessarily reflect the views of the publisher, and the publisher hereby disclaims any responsibility for them.

The author of this book does not dispense medical advice or prescribe the use of any technique as a form of treatment for physical, emotional, or medical problems without the advice of a physician, either directly or indirectly. The intent of the author is only to offer information of a general nature to help you in your quest for emotional and spiritual well-being. In the event you use any of the information in this book for yourself, which is your constitutional right, the author and the publisher assume no responsibility for your actions.

Any people depicted in stock imagery provided by Thinkstock are models, and such images are being used for illustrative purposes only. Certain stock imagery © Thinkstock.

Printed in the United States of America

Balboa Press rev. date: 7/6/2012

"A NEW SPECIES IS ARISING ON THE PLANET.

IT IS ARISING NOW,

AND YOU ARE IT!"

From Eckhart Tolle's "A New Earth"

Acknowledgments

My deep thanks and ongoing appreciation go to my many dear friends who helped birth this book in a myriad of ways. Some were terrific handholders, some read and advised well, others knew the ways of the elusive computer so much better than I, and a number of my benefactors contributed fine material to the work. And so I offer my sincere gratitude to Susan Hardman, Rusty and Sandra Stephens, Michelle Stevens and Jeffrey Swiger for their many ways of assisting.

My loving regard goes to my buddies contributing material to this book including Carole Ann Al-Din, Patricia Chirpas, Eva Fisher, Sheila Forester, Susan Hardman, Michael Kirkpatrick, John Kramer, Jill Saner, Deborah Sinclair, Rusty Stephens and Leslie Underdonks. They upgraded the book beautifully and I am very blessed by their efforts. That's a great way to write a book – get your friends to join in. Good friends are indeed one of our greatest assets in life.

And new friends joined in as well. My check-in coordinator, Adriane Pontecorvo, and my design liaison person, Jennifer Slaybaugh, must surely have wings as they have been angels to me in assisting with the preparation of this manuscript.

My MAP Team has inspired and guided me many times beyond my knowledge and imagination as well as the vast number of times when I could feel them right here assisting with the process.

Many, many thanks to all. My good fortune abounds!

Dedication

These pages are dedicated to my
beloved spouse, Herschel,
who has endured with patience and love
throughout this effort and so very many others

to my beloved parents, Max and Julia,
who always gave me the very finest of themselves

and to the Spiritual Hierarchy of this planet
without whom this would surely not exist

to all my teachers
seen and unseen
known and unknown
my deep love and gratitude

Contents

Introduction
Traveling Home Together

*M*y friends, through decades I have been blessed by encountering many spiritual paths, teachings, and practices. All encounters have born fruit but some have excelled in what they have offered me. This book is my effort to share with you what I have found to be true, useful to spiritual awakening, and producing joy and peace in myself and in many around me.

Whether the few paragraphs below speak to you or touch your Soul in any way or you simply wish to live a more serene, happier and love-filled life, this book will offer you concepts and methods to support your journey and the attainment of your goals. They are certainly doing that for me.

I want to share the experiences, concepts, and practices that have made my life much gentler and more loving. I want to share everything that I believe can help us all make our way through these times with less pain, greater success, and more ease. I want to share whatever will assist us in understanding the nature of our spiritual journey so we may enjoy the experience of our travels and the bliss that comes with the true feeling of oneness with all life.

This level of spiritual awakening requires coming to know our identity as the Divine Soul that never dies and has placed us on a mystical path which is now at a difficult crossroads. Most of us recognize that the planet and all it contains is in a very challenging transition at this point. This early part of the Twenty First Century is a critical period. Much in our world and our personal lives is in turmoil.

These are unprecedented times and very painful for many, and yet immensely filled with possibilities for our future. Our planet is being permeated with transformational energy that any and all of us can make the most of - or the least of. It is our choice. Joy does await us and will expand within us as our consciousness embraces ever-greater spiritual truth. It is our Soul's birthright; joy and love are the nature and core of our very existence. They enfold us as we remember who we truly are.

For us to rise up in our consciousness requires that we deeply examine our thoughts, emotions, words, and deeds. We must recognize those that are in our way to higher wisdom. What are our current belief systems, attachments, and desires that hold us and others down in unhappiness and fear?

To achieve this advance in insight and the resulting shift in behavior in ourselves and restore the Divine Plan on earth requires an entirely new system of ethics and values. We are invited to arise in love – to love and accept ourselves in our entirety and to recognize and experience the eternal Divinity within – and then to love our neighbors as ourselves. All creation is in our neighborhood.

We are asked to expand our vision and extend our love into a practice of sharing with all so that all are cared for. The reward that comes with that expansion is world peace and a union with all our brethren. The joy and inner fulfillment that will be ours as this comes about is beyond words. We can transform ourselves and the world. Our next chapter is entitled "The Time is Now". And it is. This is it! This is our time of living our choice, our time for healing.

My hope is that something in these pages will help us to see ourselves and the entire world from a more advanced viewpoint. It is time for us to really come together and move forward in greater light; to become a part of that "critical mass" - here a reference to the number of enlightened souls needed to tilt the scale of the world wide consciousness. A change in perspective is what is now requested and required for healing. That's the invitation being extended from above and within the depths of our being. It is an invitation extended to us all.

Most of you know the metaphor about the blind men and the elephant. I'd like to share a somewhat abbreviated form of this wisdom as I recall and interpret it. Several blind men expressed an interest in knowing what an elephant looks like. So a well-meaning individual took them to visit one. The men proceeded to feel the elephant; they used their hands to form a mental picture.

Now as the metaphor goes someone asked the men after their encounter how the elephant looked to them. They all described it somewhat differently having touched different parts of the immense creature. Some emphasized tusks, or large solid feet, tough hide, a rounded belly or the trunk. Everyone had a different image to present. A couple of them had put several parts together for their picture.

Each man felt his image to be correct and the others wrong; none understood the limitations of their singular viewpoint. Some arguing ensued. Eventually they came to comprehend that all views were needed to form a true picture of the whole. Conflict ceased and harmony descended.

That's where I think we are spiritually. We're exploring more and getting a bigger picture of what's going on in the Universe. However, few of us have a vision of the whole spiritual canvas. We're describing parts and too often think the part is the entirety. Judgment and blaming occur. Self-righteousness abounds. It can be a blessing to realize we still know so little and thus release the conflict. In these chapters I have shared the parts I have come to know. There are many more. Let's put my parts together with your parts and see what further we can grasp and become wiser.

These chapters are a myriad of shared thoughts. There is a section based on teachings that have proven themselves to me time and again for decades, leading me on to deeper stillness and awareness. There's a section on various methods of moving forward with greater ease and wholeness which have demonstrated their effectiveness to me on a daily basis for many years. And a few testimonies, stories of my experiences, and wise words from a few dear friends are thrown in here and there.

Reading the chapters in order will allow for easier connections among them but feel free to jump in anywhere that calls to you. I will address key concepts from different angles at times; repetition of important truths is very useful to not only grasping the concepts intellectually but, more importantly, taking what's right for us into our inner self and living it daily.

The phrase "what is right for us" is crucial. Please take from these pages what feels useful to you, what registers as being productive to your journey and awakening. Let's make a deal. I can share what has become higher truth and fruitful practice for me and you can choose what is right for your present process. That gives both of us a lot of freedom.

So please join me in this inner adventure. Let's ramble along this path of love and light. Allow our time together to bring you greater peace, hope, and understanding of who we truly are, what our lives are about and the enlightenment that awaits. I'd love to have your company.

Chapter 1
Now is the Time

Some time ago I offered a seminar that struck a chord in many attending. It was oriented toward reminding us to take our personal spiritual journey more seriously. I distributed a handout that contained paragraphs touching on the essentials of the journey. It was great to see the positive response attendees had to the material. Requests for further copies of these few words still come my way. As this is the beginning of our journey together, I thought I would include those words in the chance that they will offer you something as well. They are, in part, a highlighting and repetition of some of what I shared in the introduction. I am very fond of abbreviated material. Here is the content of that handout.

"Now is the time to understand our tremendous opportunity, challenge and current need of the world. Our world is in crisis while simultaneously great divine energies pour forth onto us to inspire and assist in healing ourselves and thus this crisis. We have the opportunity to take a leap forward in our personal spiritual evolution while bringing this planet into a more enlightened age.

Now is the time to remember and connect with the loving spiritual guidance and support that is available to us constantly. The Spiritual Hierarchy, consisting of Beings who have finished the human portion of their spiritual journey, never ceases to help us all move forward as we become willing. While resting in as much inner quiet as we can achieve, we are well advised to ask for that aid regularly and sincerely. We become more open to what God knows is best for all. We seldom know what needs to happen in God's plan for our enlightenment.

Now is the time to assess where we are in our spiritual development, how we nurture that development each day, and how we express our consciousness in every moment of our lives. Again, ask for assistance in developing this insight. Take a genuine and sincere inventory. Look objectively at your thoughts, your actions, and your sharing of love. How do you want to feel each day? What do you want to offer yourself and the world? Make that choice! Our primary goal as human beings is to awaken. Do we reach for inspiration daily to support this process? I ask myself these questions frequently.

Now is the time to commit to a reasonable course of action that accelerates our being our true Self. Most of us know very well the difference in how we feel and what we give to others when we take those moments to meditate, pray, read what inspires us, or just breathe into the Now. We are fully capable of choosing how much Divine Light we draw into ourselves and our lives.

Now is the time to serve all life through our every thought, feeling, word and deed. When we nurture our spiritual connection, we are contributing to world healing. It is a needed service to simply observe our thoughts and keep them aligned with higher understanding and compassion. When our thoughts are wise and loving, all the rest falls into place. We become joyful!

Speaking of abbreviated material, on this page I include a summary of these main points.

Many have placed these in a spot where they will see them often. We need reminders.

NOW IS THE TIME. . .

TO REMEMBER THAT THIS IS AN AGE OF
GREAT SPIRITUAL OPPORTUNITY,

TO RECALL THAT DIVINE SPIRITUAL
ASSISTANCE IS OURS AT ALL TIMES AND MAKE
GREATER USE OF THAT CONNECTION,

TO STAY IN TOUCH WITH HOW
WE SPIRITUALLY NURTURE OURSELVES EACH DAY,

TO COMMIT TO GREATER EFFORT TOWARD THIS
NURTURING OF OUR SOUL UNION, AND

TO RECOGNIZE ALWAYS WHAT A
SERVICE THIS EFFORT IS
TO THE HEALING OF THE ENTIRE WORLD.

Chapter 2
Introduction to Part I
Spiritual Thought to Heal and Nourish our Hearts and Minds

*I*n my childhood and youth, I was depressed and very fearful. I remember when first attending school, I tried to hide in the enclosed bottom of my little desk as though if my head were hidden, no one would know I was there. I grew up in the country until the age of eleven and, being an only child, had no other children around. So I really was very unsure in first grade what these other little people were all about and how to interact with them. It was very scary to me and I was not off to a good start.

It wasn't until my high school years that I began to emerge from my fearful shell. As I ventured through college and graduate school, I still often felt sad, anxious, and unworthy. My darkness peaked in my late twenties while on a vacation. I remember sitting in a strange room, alone, and struggling to make sense of myself and life and feeling things closing in on me. I'm sure at least a few of you can identify with some of that dismay and confusion. Many of us have been there.

For no reason I could grasp suddenly the entire room turned the brightest gold I had ever seen. It was glorious to behold - thrilling in truth. It was electrical and powerful and permeated every part of me. I think it only lasted a few minutes but when the Light disappeared, I felt very different. It turned out that I was very different. I really didn't know what to make of it and didn't have the wisdom to attribute it to any divine source at that point. I'm surely not saying I have had no sad and anxious days since then but in those few minutes I sharply turned a corner.

Within months, I was drawn to meditation. And gradually through the following years I encountered quite a variety of spiritual teachings, practices, and experiences. Some long ago have been put aside with gratitude for what they have offered me and some have remained life-long friends and become an essential part of who I am.

I had majored in Philosophy and World Theology in college (always a great job getter) and had completed that experience with much spiritual uncertainty. But now as the years went by, my sense of what Higher Power, God or Universal Source meant to me became clearer. The experience of the Divinity of us all continues to be brought into my heart daily. Having that experience of our Oneness in God has made all the difference. It is true; God is love! And at our core, our true Self, we are that love as well.

So here is Part I which is a focus on the many teachings that have genuinely changed my life and have continued to be those life-long friends. We have in these pages discussions of spiritual belief systems, some thoughts from a few others who have enjoyed the same wonderful effects that I have, and a few more experiences thrown in for good measure.

I surely hope something shared here will speak to you! I hope your Soul will tap you on the shoulder somewhere through the pages and say "hey, buddy, this one is for you"! And I surely anticipate some chuckles as we go! Just leave behind what's not for you. I again welcome you to join me on this our very own form of "walkabout".

Chapter 3
Serenity Plus in Five Stages

*M*ost of us feel that serenity is one of our true goals. We want inner peace! We want tranquility and calm! We often ache with the desire to change the content of our minds and to have more control over our thoughts. This can only be achieved if we continue to make efforts to nourish ourselves spiritually through making daily advances in changing how we view ourselves, others, and the world. Never before has there been a greater need for us to quicken our process, for us to enhance our own spiritual awakening and bring greater light into our minds and the world. In these following stages a pathway lies that most of us take on our journey into serenity.

1. THE STAGE OF SPIRITUAL UNCONSCIOUSNESS

We may still have our moments in this unaware stage but most of us choosing to read a book such as this have already achieved some degree of understanding that there are more spiritually advanced ways of viewing who we are and all that takes place. However, remembering the many times we have behaved in this unconsciousness may open us to greater compassion for those who have not awakened from this ego-dominated state of mind. We've all been there.

2. THE STAGE OF BEGINNING TO AWAKEN TO HIGHER REALITIES

It is a blessed time when we begin to expand our view of what our lives are all about. Here are some examples of concepts that move us through these stages more quickly and start to take root in our conscious mind in this stage 2.

We're becoming somewhat familiar with the Law of Attraction. We can attract experiences to ourselves through our ego desires and reactions or through our Soul connection. Either way, every inner and outer experience that comes our way can be used by Higher Power to assist us in our spiritual evolution. Now we may begin to believe that the more enduring aspects of our lives we have agreed to before birth, at that time knowing their possibilities for our awakening. We all have "soul contracts" for what we will experience and hopefully choose to learn in each life as the well-known author Caroline Myss so beautifully reminds us. That is one of my favorite phrases from her many fine works.

We may begin to be attracted to some form of meditation. Any meditation period reflected on with care shows us that many of our thoughts are judgments in some form. An endless sequence of events and persons, including ourselves, are not satisfactory to us in numerous ways – past, present, and future. We condemn; we criticize in our minds. Thus one way of gaining further serenity is to mentally slow down and really examine the nature of our thoughts. Usually we will see through many of them as possible fallacies built on lack of wisdom and reflective awareness. Knowing we don't know all we thought we knew can be a great relief! Recognizing our ignorance actually can be blissful. How quiet within we can become when we diminish those many fearful, condemning and attacking thoughts that are all based on some form of judging.

So how do we diminish those judging thoughts and gain more serenity? We can consider the following ideas. We are most assuredly not all at the same level of awakening. Metaphorically speaking, we are not all in the same grade of earth's spiritual school. We're not all working with the same knowledge, experiences, insights, motives, and connection to our own Soul. There need be no judgment of that fact; we're simply not all of the same spiritual age so to speak. A question to ask is do we expect the same mature behavior from a first grader as we do from a high school student?

Thus, from *A Course in Miracles* the statement that everyone is doing the best they can with what they currently have to work with has tremendous validity. I probably rely on that the most in all my moments of showing a lack of wisdom. I am now better at moving past the stage of the self-recriminations and guilt. What are they saying these days? "If we knew better, we'd do better." I see that as being true. And feeling guilty doesn't help us improve. Seeing our errors, asking for Divine assistance with them, and committing to doing better does!

I just love the material that emphasizes whatever has upset us the most today is our finest teacher of the day. That means that our negative emotional reactions point to unhealed aspects of our psyche as hard as that usually is to consider. And without that pointer, we often remain unaware of a wound, a part of ourselves that needs our loving and healing attention. Believe it or not, we are actually able to witness negative behavior and circumstances without being emotionally upset as our wisdom about the worldly school increases. That does not make us passive. It allows our interventions to have greater vision and more loving effectiveness in them.

I can see error in myself or another and offer a blessing of love or I can dump negative emotions on that error and pollute myself and the world even further. We can assess a situation without judging or condemning it. No inner uproar, just quiet. That takes real work, some solid inner development that comes with ongoing inner examination. As a result of our efforts producing increased calm and centeredness, what we do tends to be for the better.

So what if this is all true? We are doing the best we can with what we've got and we've agreed to the experiences we have in life and for good purpose. We know that most of our learning comes through the difficult times, and we know that God does not condemn us as God knows well that awakening involves a lot of mistakes along the way. What if you believed just a portion of this? Can you see the potential that this wisdom has for giving us a serene, more loving and understanding mind and life? It can be truly altering to our consciousness! These are some of the ideas that likely begin to take shape in stage 2. Don't concern yourself if they don't sit well now. We'll be examining these concepts in more detail in the chapters ahead. We'll have plenty of time for reflection.

3. THE STAGE OF REMEMBERING SPIRITUAL TRUTH AFTER AN UNCONSCIOUS RESPONSE

However much of this type of thinking we adopt, we will go through a stage where we still sometimes act before we think. We'll act out an old typical response as a result of our usual ego thinking and then later some truth will come to us and we'll know we've been caught by the lower self beliefs again. Don't waste time in guilt. That's how it goes. Just ask for higher help in healing the ego pain and fear that causes these reactions and aim for better next time. This is quite a process. We must be patient and compassionate with all, certainly ourselves.

How terrific it is that we have even noticed that we have acted from our ego viewpoint and then remembered a more loving and advanced understanding. What a breakthrough! And if needed, this allows us to make amends for any of our wrongful reactions that took place before we remembered the higher truth of the situation.

4. THE STAGE OF REMEMBERING SPIRITUAL TRUTH BEFORE WE ACT

Now it becomes truly gratifying. Gradually we are becoming more immediately aware of our thoughts, feelings, and actions. We're remembering our higher perspective much more quickly. We've been fostering it and acting from greater love and wisdom. It feels terrific at those moments. Another huge chunk of peace has just dropped into our hearts due to our good efforts. Initially the ego may start its inner dialogue leading to judgment and negative behavior, but our wisdom steps in and takes the lead. Our Higher Self is on a roll.

Our ego is less and less in control any longer and we have embedded the higher truths deeply within and they come to our aid when needed. That is much of the time in this stage. It is not just our actions that result from our enlightened behavior, but we additionally have the peace of our enlightened thought and feeling. Through this spiritual awareness, our relationships improve in quality and contentment as well. We have less conflict in our lives and within ourselves.

5. THE STAGE OF THE SERENE MIND WHEN HIGHER KNOWLEDGE IS FULLY INGRAINED

This is now true inner peace. Slowly it all has become firmly grounded within and there is no effort for us to feel joyful and centered. It is a wonderfully elevated state. We simply know, through and through, that the process of awakening is enhanced in ourselves; we bless and love all, and we become a ray of light on this path forward. We are serene even in the face of very difficult times-our own and those of the world.

I can vividly recall the first time I witnessed a rather horrific act and immediately felt compassion and love for all involved. I wasn't excusing fearful and erroneous behavior. I was offering the only response that could bring true healing and correction – love and understanding wisely extended. It was an immense joy to me in that very moment to experience that genuine recognition that we are all children of God. It is not a constant state for me yet. However, it will be for all of us in the future.

That's when we are most powerful to affect the change that is required for our earth's transition into a finer dimension. That is where we are all headed, my friends; slow but sure. By fostering our wisdom and peace, we do quicken the process, perhaps a great deal. So what do we do now to facilitate this growth? Well, that's what all these following chapters are about – attaining the state of mind described here. However, I will share a few brief thoughts on this growth process now. It's never too early to increase our efforts.

I could never speak too highly of regular meditation whether it be daily at home or with local groups. Meditation is mind training of the finest form. We not only see the fallacies our minds are constantly churning up, but we additionally learn not to allow them to control us. We gradually identify less with our thoughts and feelings; we come to know they are not part of our true identity. And we are developing ever greater Soul union as well. We have much material ahead on this topic.

Additionally you might keep close one or more favorite spiritual books which really speak to you. Read portions every day; make it a commitment, even if it is just fifteen minutes. On your iPad, PC or paper briefly write the essence of several spiritual understandings that alter your thinking and bring you back to your Soul Self. Review and add to these truths every day. Whip them out when the ego starts to rant. We must reprogram our minds to Higher Reality, the actual Divine Truth about ourselves and our spiritual process. It is our responsibility to do so. We are all Divine Eternal Beings! We must support ourselves in feeling and expressing that Divinity.

In the following chapters we will get into these beliefs and practices in more detail as I mentioned. Please consider what is right for you. We will move into this greater serenity as we proceed on this path. Peace for us all is there for the taking.

Chapter 4
Spiritual Thoughts that
are Miracles in my Life

*T*here are references to this magnificent and challenging spiritual work in several places throughout this book. These concepts have played a significant role in transforming my consciousness for over thirty years. Several of the ideas in the last chapter are Course inspired. Many of you may be familiar with *A Course in Miracles*. However, let me share a few introductory words about this wonderful book.

It was scribed by Helen Schucman during the 1960s and 1970s and published in 1976. When she inquired who was this Source speaking to her, she was told it was Jesus. Now that may put some folks off immediately. However through the years much inspiring and wise material has been given by advanced beings to those of us who are receptive. My motto for everything I read or hear is that I listen reflectively for what is or is not beneficial to my growth. I skip the step of judging the source. God can speak through any of us if desired.

Helen was further told that the Course was offered to remind us of our Divine Eternal Being, our ever-loving God who does not punish, and that true Forgiveness is meant to be learned by all. The Course speaks to us about awakening to the love that we all are and releasing our fear, our greatest hindrance to Soul unity. It is a powerful manuscript that offers healing and peace to one and all. It states that it is given us as a correction to many religious misunderstandings of today.

Most of the concepts in the Course to my knowledge are likewise found in other spiritual works. I value hearing teachings not only repetitively but also phrased and presented differently. For me, this repetition and varied presentation rounds out my understanding and supports my using this knowledge in everyday life. I need to review great teachings again and again to make it all come alive throughout my being and behavior.

Let us never underestimate how important it is to study the same truths over and over. I have books, CDs, and DVDs that I have reviewed dozens of times through the years, each time gaining new insights. Having intellectual knowledge of a principle is one phase of learning. Starting to believe it, if it feels right to us, is our next step. Then it can be quite a span of time as we gradually implement this knowledge in our thoughts, feelings, and actions. And that's what is necessary to truly move ahead in our spiritual awareness – really grasping higher truth and living it deep inside.

"Miracles", as the word is used in the Course, refers to a spontaneous change in our understanding of what is true. These "miracles" gradually enhance our shift in consciousness. They can sometimes seem to appear out of nowhere and just pop into our mind at a strategic moment. They are a shift in our comprehension of higher realities and how they play out in our lives. And they are often called "miracle moments". They are filled with grace and are Divine gifts. These are the miracles the Course offers us.

Perhaps you have had the experience of your eternal Self. That feeling can spring up at any time under any circumstance for any of us. That is a high-powered "miracle moment". However, putting effort into cultivating that knowledge and experience is highly productive. When we finally get who we all really are, how we see everything changes dramatically as I've highlighted before. The Course is invaluable to this process.

It presents to us the truth that we are not only a body and personality and invites us to never be bamboozled into thinking of ourselves or others as simply that. This body/mind aspect of us is just a temporary package used for learning in this world. One of our world's great sages of the past, Pierre Teilhard de Chardin reminded us that "we are not physical beings having a spiritual experience but spiritual beings having a physical experience." Ah!

We do need this body and personality to fulfill our learning goals for this lifetime; therefore they are highly valuable vehicles which require care and nourishment so that our process is successful. Remember we have agreed to the general plan of experience in this life in league with our Soul, knowing at that point before re-entry into this world what circumstances, happenings, and people will give us the best opportunity for spiritually waking up in the most expeditious fashion. We may take full advantage of those circumstances or not, but the plan is there to benefit us as fully as possible.

Additional terms frequently used in the Course deserve some definition. "Awakening" or "waking up" is a wonderful reminder that we already have ultimate truth within us but it has been covered over by our egos. Our task here is to remove our inner obstacles to remembering who we are and what the journey is about. And we gradually do, which is "awakening".

The term "ego" in the Course refers to the belief system of the world which we have adopted. It includes our acceptance that our fulfillment, peace, and happiness lie in our making outer circumstances what we wish them to be. So we scurry through our lives trying to fulfill these wrongful expectations that seldom offer us what we think we want more than briefly. The Course moves us along toward release of the ego belief system which quickly changes the level of serenity in our lives. We are invited to consider that our inner connection with God and our eternal Self is the only true source of our ultimate fulfillment.

I cannot overestimate the help I have received through remembering the Course statement that we have no idea what lies in our own best interests. We know what our ego finds appealing and comfortable, but that usually has little connection to what takes us into enlightenment as quickly as possible. That is what is in our best interests. This helps me see through my ego desires much more quickly. Remembering I don't know what is best for my own or anyone's awakening unburdens me greatly.

Advanced studies emphasize becoming more detached from our own personal desires and wants. "Not my will but Thine" sums up an ultimate goal and expresses the knowledge that we truly do not know what serves our spiritual needs to the fullest. This surrender can be accomplished with greater facility as we proceed with our own inner healing. As long as we believe our fulfillment lies outside of us, detachment and surrender are very difficult. Pain and disappointment are easily attained.

Many of us have commented through the years that we surrender situations to God and then often, if we are paying enough attention to notice, we try to take back the control due to our fear of what God may do with it. Sister Rose, one of our most beloved and long time Course students, would remind us of this process that never failed to help us see how difficult it is to truly surrender to that Higher Power. How our egos want things to work out and what truly is the Divine best are very different scenarios.

I love the Course's idea that it is impossible for the entire world to share one religious perspective. However it goes on to say that what is important and entirely possible is for each individual to go beyond the mind and experience God's love. That is an ultimate goal and these concepts assist us in making that leap, in creating a conscious desire and ability in us to receive that healing experience. It is entirely beyond intellect; it truly is a matter of our heart and Soul.

The Course advises us that we are invited to always ask for Divine help. We need to realize we are never alone. We need to learn to call out for assistance in any and all ways. When we do this, attention, love, guidance, and support will be given us. We may or may not recognize and appreciate the form it comes in. Another saying I hear a lot these days is "every prayer is answered; we just may not like the answer". This reminds us that we don't know what is best for us in the bigger picture.

The central concept in the Course is that of Forgiveness. I capitalize Forgive because here this word takes on a superlative meaning far beyond how we normally think of this idea. We're presented with the truth that nothing ever happens that requires Forgiveness; that everything has opportunity, meaning, and purpose in it even though we don't usually recognize that there is a Divine Plan playing out. This is often a very objectionable idea to many and quickly disposed of, but yet has such great power to change us. This concept deserves a chapter devoted to it alone. Remembering that we often learn the most from our mistakes adds a bit more acceptability to this belief.

And in my reverence to repetition I say again we are here to remember who we truly are, that Divine Eternal Being of great love. I continually repeat that because so few of us believe it; so few of us really feel this deep inside. However, realizing that truth gives us freedom from our fear, our anger, our despair, our anxiety, and from all of those ego responses that bring misery to our lives and those around us changes us.

That state of mind is beyond thought, beyond concepts. Spiritual truths and witnessing our thoughts, beliefs, and feelings are steps toward that beyond. The Course, while offering us many useful conceptual steps, is at its finest an invitation to go beyond the mind into pure awareness. That is the ultimate goal of all meditation, all spiritual study, and all of life.

These few paragraphs are the tiniest of smatterings of the many concepts, understandings and encouragement that the Course offers us in page after page. It is very well worth investigating and there are many hundreds of thousands of people studying this world-wide as well as there being many study groups. It became well known and subsequently treasured by many after Oprah Winfrey richly brought it to our attention some years ago.

To begin your study a little more lightly if you wish, you might consider the books of Marianne Williamson devoted to the Course: *A Return to Love* and *The Gift of Change* both valued by so many. Those of Paul Ferrini also have been favorites. Both Marianne's and Paul's books are gentler ways to initially approach the Course. Two other current books that my Course buddies really value are *Daily Meditations for Practicing the Course* by Karen Casey and *Spirit Junkie: A Radical Road to Self-Love and Miracles* by Gabrielle Bernstein. They are good current avenues for uplifting exploration of these teachings.

If you have interest in the Course's concept of this world being an illusion, a very challenging and worthwhile teaching, Gary Renard's books are gems. They are fascinating! I just loved them. Dr. Jon Mundy's works as well as those of Dr. Kenneth Wapnick are somewhat more advanced and immensely worthy of our study. I have learned a great deal from those and continue to do so. I read and reread many passages in these as they are very healing and uplifting.

The Course, although couched in many common Christian terms, is not of any specific religion. It can be inviting and inspiring to those of any religious persuasion or spiritual perspective. I am reminded here of the Dalai Lama's statement, when asked, that his religion was kindness. How the world would be immediately transformed if we could all adopt that faith.

Chapter 5
Living the Peace of True Forgiveness

*A*ll of us, to some degree, are affected by guilt, anger, fear, despair, blaming, a sense of victimization and a further host of painful emotions that arise from our lack of understanding the nature of our journey.

Most of us know these days that any and all negative thoughts and feelings are a detriment to our bodily functioning. From our immune system to our strength level, there is no end to the weakening that takes place throughout our body when our emotions, thoughts, and beliefs are of a wounded and painful nature. And that's to say nothing of the emotional distress that we live with as we continue to be burdened with unforgiveness for ourselves and others. Many folks work on forgiveness, by any understanding of the word, simply to relieve themselves of these self-injurious emotions.

Maybe this is as good a place as any to toss in this metaphor related to guilt and judgment and the associated pain. I've used this image for self-examination many times and with many clients through the years.

Let's pretend for a moment that all our despair, anxiety, or misery related to something in our lives is twelve inches deep. What I have quite often found in myself and others is that the first four to six inches of the pain is connected to the initial event or circumstance. It may be something we or another have done. Or it can be our own depression or anxiety that plagues us. The possibilities for what is initially troubling us are endless.

However the remaining number of the twelve inches is usually made up of anger, guilt, or judgment of some variety that we are feeling related to the first few inches, and it is directed toward ourselves. In other words, we feel something painful; that should be a sufficient burden for us. But then we go on to judge ourselves for feeling that. "Why can't I just get over this?" "Why do I let this take such control of me?" "What a wuss I am for not just shaking this off!" And on it goes.

Frequently I work with people to identify the content of their twelve inches; the self-judgmental part on them is what gets tackled first. Very often, when folks are asked to really examine what they are saying to themselves about their condition or reaction, they can begin to see some fallacy in that assessment within a matter of a few hard working weeks. They can lighten up on themselves with some insight.

I often ask them if they would judge someone else equally harshly in similar circumstances. Their answer is often "no". Sometimes I'll tell them a similar story to their own about myself or another and we'll look deeply at what they feel about that. It is so different than what they lay on themselves. This can reduce a person's emotional distress even by half. And it's the concepts in this chapter and chapters 4 and 6 that often allow them to forgive themselves and take a new perspective.

Is this making sense? Sometimes a goodly portion of our distress is our lack of forgiveness for our not being able to handle something in a better way. This assessment is very often not rational or reasonable. We can change that. I'm reminded of numerous people I've worked with who on a regular basis attacked themselves in thought and even behavior for their inability to deal with some initial problem, thus doubling their difficulties and pain. We can stop doing this!

This twelve inch metaphor can apply to a vast number of circumstances. A situation or condition or person is troubling to us and then we make it twice as difficult or upsetting with our irrational thoughts. We usually think they are rational but under closer scrutiny, they are often negative biases arising from past experiences projecting into the present or future. We can affect ourselves and situations quite adversely through our negative assessments. Again we double our trouble. We're loaded with all-or-nothing thinking or predicting scenarios or always expecting the worst. Investigating the content of our own minds on any issue can offer much relief to our miseries. It is the thoughts we have about any situation that determine its effect on us; listen closely to your mind. See through your negativity and pessimism and past training to get to the simple and actual facts of your situation. We all have our share of falsely-based beliefs.

A woman I was seeing in therapy recently is illustrative of so many of us. She had just gone through a very trying divorce, had small children and was very uneasy and afraid. She frequently entertained thoughts that she would always be alone and would never find anyone to share her life with as a partner due to all her judged inadequacies. She would then go further into the darkness believing her children would never do well due to not having a healthy male influence. And on it went.

Her actual situation was certainly difficult enough, however the added negative beliefs were crippling to her. She was quite intelligent though and within a short time she was able to see that her dismal "futurizing" (I think I made that up) was based on her own childhood experiences. She did a fine job of casting these expectations aside over several months of effort and was much more capable of managing her current circumstances well. And, of course, additionally she was much less depressed and anxious. We can all think of our own examples of negative thinking and we, too, can cast irrational perspectives aside. Even though sometimes lack of forgiveness is hard to pick up on in our many negative thoughts, it is present more often than most of us would think. It takes many forms.

When I think of the first six inches of our difficulties or, for that matter, all of our challenges and pains, I remember so many great beings saying that suffering has a divine cause. Suffering gradually burns away our ego desires and expands our consciousness. Without suffering, in its many forms, we would not move forward in our awakening. And that reminds me of our upcoming chapter on gratitude. We do come to value our learning experiences, even those filled with woes. Then everything feels lighter.

For the remainder of this chapter, I invite you to suspend your judgment on the principles I'll share and just make some space within yourself for "let's pretend". Let's pretend that these ideas have truth to them and imagine how you might feel if you adopted any one or all of them in your daily life. Let's just see how that would affect you and if you might be greatly unburdened. We're now heading into the capital F Forgiveness zone.

Forgiveness is the central concept and challenge of the Course as I mentioned. I capitalize it because this form is quite different from our normal understanding of what forgiveness means. This Forgiveness has the power to offer us greater peace and joy than we can imagine. True Course Forgiveness is defined as awakening so fully to the ways of the Universe that we come to know that nothing that takes place requires any Forgiveness. Initially almost all of us reject such a notion and find it quite objectionable. But what are the truths that this seemingly outlandish statement is based on? Is it possible we actually believe some of them even now?

Some of these concepts are commonplace to us. Loads of folks who would choose reading material like this already believe that there is meaning, purpose, and plan to the events in their lives. That's a lot easier to say than to apply when the chips are down. But deeper investigation often lends us a hand.

A part of my psychotherapy practice through the years has been to utilize hypnotic-like processes that invite my clients to move into an altered state of awareness. We only utilize this aid when we both deem it likely to be useful and it is part of an ongoing process of healing. And we have done our best to receive higher guidance on doing so. It is an invitation to access our own deeper dimensions and awareness with the assistance of loving Divine Beings.

I wouldn't want to call this a regression technique as I am very careful not to suggest our destination for our inner adventure, but rather we specify what we seek. It is actually very therapeutic for us to thoughtfully define exactly what we are hoping to learn and heal, and what we wish to discover. So we might phrase our request in terms of moving to a dimension of awareness that will shed light on whatever the concern may be. For example we request the guidance and assistance of those Divine Beings present, including our own Soul of course, to allow us access to the memories or knowledge that will best accomplish a particular healing. We know today the important power of intention. We need to know what we want and why; this needs to be clear in our minds.

The process then may land us in any of quite a variety of places. We may access something in a past, present, or future life. We may spend time in a "life-between-life" experience, a time of evaluation and planning before we enter this life. Maybe our own Soul or a Guide or our MAP Team (see chapter 26) might speak with us; they may talk with us about what we are seeking. It is very important that we remain in the Light and Love of God throughout this experience to remain pure in our results. It is easy to fool ourselves. The outcome of the work often proves the validity of the experience, the changes that take place in people when greater knowledge is now theirs.

A number of my clients, who have engaged in this altered state process, have accessed a dimension in which they have been shown the meaning of the suffering and trauma of their lives. And many have learned that all they have been through was agreed to by their Soul in Its great wisdom. In some cases, it has been agreed to because it is a training experience for what they are being prepared for in their future.

I recall one person who had indeed suffered greatly and lived in deep depression and anger, feeling understandably very much the victim. In our session he was shown how his experiences were to be used in a future time to help many others. He saw how every wound and loss would blossom into wisdom, compassion, and understanding that would not only direct his healing work with many others, but additionally that work would bring him a joy and peace he had never known. This experience felt so indelibly true to him that it changed his perspective on his entire life. It all had purpose and meaning to him now. He was and is a new man! And his experience is not unique. Others have traveled this path as well.

In fact his tale is the tale of us all. We may never consciously know at this time what the meaning of our experiences is. However, I assure you that this is the nature of our journey. We are offered, by the choice of our Soul, ongoing opportunities to learn what we are meant to learn, to remember what is buried deep inside. For many of us the greatest pain brings the greatest knowing and reward in the end.

Pain and difficulty, of course, are not our only paths of learning and remembering. When we truly begin to wake up, we will choose experiences offering us deeper inner wisdom and awareness that do not include hard times. Wise choices can develop from our present Soul connection as well as from challenging circumstances and events.

In some of my "altered state" work, people have moved to their "planning stage" that took place right before dropping back into this world for another round. There are some very good books available discussing this type of work. A book entitled *Life Between Life* by Joel Whitton, M.D comes to mind. Exciting stuff!

This "planning stage" awareness can easily shift our view of our own life's mosaic pattern. I feel my life has been a rather strange one with many oddities and surprises. When I underwent this work myself and was given a much bigger picture of what I was meant to be all about and what I had pledged to accomplish in this life, so much made a great deal more sense and was easier to accept. I had often blamed myself for being such an oddball of sorts and not fitting into a conventional mode of life. After this increased insight was given me, I released the condemnation and have continued to feel much more comfortable in myself and my patterns of life.

So in this altered state of planning people see that we have agreed to most of the circumstances and happenings of our lives. We may or may not already have this belief but the experience takes that truth to a much deeper and more healing level. Life is rather perfectly organized; not perfectly for our ego comforts and desires, but rather perfectly for the opportunity of awakening to the truth as quickly as possible. This now becomes a more firm understanding for them.

You may have noticed I said "most of" our life's pattern we have agreed to. Let us not forget we do have a measure of free will at the lower self level. Egos make some poor choices and we create some chaos for ourselves that isn't necessary. This is acceptable as well because that's just another type of learning experience that can take us ahead. Everything is used to our benefit if we are willing within. No one makes all the inspired choices all the time.

These poor choices make a strong case however for developing Forgiveness skills. At times in altered state work people have discovered some wrong turns they have chosen in this or another life. If they don't have the big picture, they can drop into further guilt, anger and pain. Or they may see the wrongs of others and have very negative reactions. Adopting these more progressive belief systems allows us to cope with the transgressions of this or another life with greater ease. The Course teaching coming up is a great example of what assists us in this.

This concept we touched on earlier strongly underlies true Forgiveness. It is the idea that given all our circumstances, we're all doing the best we can at any given moment. This is another idea we often reject rather swiftly. We usually can make quite a list of people and circumstances in which we are sure that no one was doing their best. I think very few people buy into this one but let's play with it a bit.

"Given all our circumstances" is a very loaded phrase. None of us know all our own past experiences let alone those of anyone else. We have no idea what all we have been through. We have no idea what occurrences have come our way and are far from healed yet, or what difficult situations we have created for others. We actually know very little.

Our current stresses and strains and how extensive our subconscious wounds may be are major players in how well we cope on any given day. What lesson we are working on at any particular time is often unknown. And Eckhart Tolle reminds us of our "pain body", that reservoir of past agonies, injuries and sorrows which affects us mightily on frequent occasions. All this and more influence how best we can deal with any given event.

I find great merit in the "grade in school" metaphor. I reiterate: we are all in different grades in our earth education. We don't expect the same behavior from a third grader as we do from an eleventh grader. They don't know the same things; they haven't had the same degree of experience; they don't have the same level of development. We don't know what grade anyone is in. That helps me to grab hold of the recommendation that we not judge ourselves or others. We simply don't have the data to correctly do the job.

Now judging isn't the same as assessing a situation and seeking guidance for appropriate action. We all must do some level of assessing daily. Do I talk to that person about their irritating behavior? Do I take that job or maintain that friendship? And on and on it goes. Judging is when we condemn a person, perhaps put them out of our hearts and maybe even hope for tough things to come their way. Judging is deciding that someone, ourselves or another, is unworthy or much more worthy, as inferior or superior, and lower or higher in God's eyes and our own. We do it all the time; we know that. But we do it unwisely with insufficient knowledge. We have no idea what God has any of us working on in this particular lifetime. We don't know what kind of balancing of karma is taking place. Remember karma is learning, not punishment.

And, of course, we do it while being drawn again into just looking at the person as the body and personality. We have forgotten the inner Divinity we all share. We will continue to do this as long as we believe our own wellbeing relies on outer circumstances rather than our inner Divine wholeness. We think our peace and joy depend on how well our ego desires are being served, so naturally we are inclined to do some serious judging when things don't go the way we think they should. It's all lower self thinking and feeling.

When many of the advanced teachings of this world advise us to not judge, I don't believe we're just being told it's not a good thing to do. I think we're being told we're totally incapable of it with any wisdom whatsoever.

We see this growing understanding reflected in such statements today as "reject the sin and love the sinner" or "give consequences to the child's poor behavior but do not condemn the child".

A number of my parenting and grand-parenting friends have adopted statements with the children such as "you are better than this; this behavior is beneath you; you are way too good for this". And when said with sincerity and love, it often has excellent impact. These statements are true for every single one of us in terms of our ego behavior, no matter what age we are. In truth we are all too good in whom we really are for the many decisions and behaviors our egos choose.

So here we have a few concepts that might slow us down in our quick judgments. Here we have spiritual perspective that makes Forgiving much more accessible to us. Releasing our judging and condemning thoughts and behaviors is one of the results of understanding that we are all doing the best we can at any given moment, even though our best may be rather poor at that time. Again, this is a concept few can easily grasp and apply in their lives. However, it is immensely rewarding to continue the effort.

Let us cultivate this more gentle and loving approach to all things. Recently I heard an interview with Sylvia Boorstein, a well-known Jewish Buddhist author, teacher and psychotherapist. She said that when she is stressed and upset, she will say to herself "Sweetheart, you are in pain. Relax. Breathe. You will work this out." That entire statement is a treasure and represents a compassionate and supportive response that we can apply to ourselves and others.

However for me the best gem is the word "Sweetheart". Isn't that just beautiful? For us to begin to think of ourselves and others genuinely in that way is so very healing and nurturing. I will admit I've used many less kindly words on myself far too many times. I am adopting that word. Down deep we are all sweet hearts; our hearts are good and loving once the burden of the ego is removed.

Now my husband says he can't quite make it to the "sweetheart" word. It is just a touch too feminine for him. So he is using "Hey, Buddy," and so forth, said increasingly with genuine affection and compassion. Cool! A very nice adaptation.

Here are a few more thoughts in support of Forgiveness. As I have said none of us knows what earth lesson our Divine Source has us working on at any given time or particular life. Many of these lessons are very demanding and challenging. We might be getting what we're supposed to get, but suffering so in the process that we are not behaving in a way that others, or perhaps ourselves, can understand or respect.

Decades ago I remember reading one of Shakti Gawain's books wherein she discussed, in metaphor form, a vital understanding. She said karma (the golden rule or what goes around, comes around) may gently whisper in our ear initially that something in particular in our thinking or behavior needs our attention. Usually we don't consciously hear that or choose not to. So with love, karma at some point comes back around and taps us strongly on the shoulder and says more loudly to pay attention to that unhealed aspect of ourselves. At some level we hear it but find lots of reasons to put off making the suggested changes. Then finally karma, again with love and patience, whacks us a good one often bringing us to our knees and says to definitely do it now!!!! It's a super point.

What I'm about to write isn't going to fit here exactly but, in my mind, it is connected to Shakti's metaphor about how we can get nudged or knocked to the ground. And it just happened a few minutes ago so I'm sticking it in. Our mailbox is out on the main road and ants regularly get in there, build a home and lay their eggs. Hersch, in his kindness to the mail lady, kills them so they won't get all over her hand when she puts the mail in, let alone the hassle of bringing ants into the house with the mail.

I have a heavy dose of harmlessness in me that I do carry too far at times. However I don't think this is one of those times. I don't like to kill the ants unnecessarily; so when I go to the mailbox and find ants there, I give them an earthquake. I beat on the mailbox and they pick up their eggs and scurry off. Stressed indeed but alive and well. To me that beats poisoning them. I offer the lesser trauma to have them avoid the more serious one.

Another example I have used for years as a metaphor for us humans not understanding what's really going on is taking our pets to the vet. They carry on like they are being severely tortured but we know we do this to save them even further difficulties. I think that is true of us kids. We go through some very hard times but it is often so that we will learn what's needed to avoid even further agonies. And usually we just feel victimized since we don't grasp the reasons behind the occurrences; we have no big picture.

Thus we are always doing the best we can which on occasion isn't so great. We may not have any understanding of what is really going on, like the ants and the pets. Maybe the pressure is intense and we're stretched to the limit from within, without or both. I may have handled something much better just last week than I am now. This week life's demands may be much greater and I'm struggling to just get through. Many truly difficult experiences come our way from the love of our Soul. We are advised to frequently ask for help, guidance and support from above and make room within ourselves for that help to arrive and be utilized well.

I delight in the fact that most of us, if asked, can recall one or many occurrences in our lives that we thought at the time were just pure hell or at least pretty awful and now we insightfully see how much we have grown and learned from the experience. To reiterate, the Course says we don't know wherein lies our own best interest. I repeat that to myself frequently. We don't have a clue what experiences are going to take us ahead in significant ways in our awakening. We know what we like and want. We don't know in most cases what our true purpose is in life. We don't know the possible outcome of any happening in our lives. Arriving at acceptance of that reality should really slow down our judgments and speed up our Forgiveness.

Thinking again of that interview with Sylvia Boorstein, I loved a metaphor she used for gentle redirection when we are tempted to condemn ourselves for something. She likened a proper calm and understanding response to ourselves to her GPS. When she is off course, the GPS voice peacefully and simply says "recalculate". No fanfare, just a serene statement. The Course's similar suggestion is to just "choose again". We get better and better at that as we take in these higher viewpoints and cease to waste time on the guilt.

The Course is very clear that at some point we all get "Home" again. It states that, at the Soul level, we have never left that bliss of union with God and it's just a matter of awakening out of this level of consciousness to experience "Home" again. "The Kingdom of God is Within" – remember that one? That's the goal; there's our peace, that's "Home".

Speaking of quickly dismissed ideas, another concept that is meaningful to me is that we have no idea how very beautiful a truly Forgiven world is. I've seen glimpses of that state of mind. And it is our state of mind that allows such true, higher vision. It's a joy beyond compare. When we fully grasp the purpose of this existence, the underlying beauty of it all, in its intricacies and complexities, it will truly take us into the bliss that is our rightful heritage.

It's very hard to imagine this present-day world as beautiful, especially with inadequate Forgiveness skills. It is only in seeing beyond the surface circumstances and the ego's activity that this great perfection becomes apparent. A quote from the Buddha that sends my heart dancing is "when you realize how perfect everything is, you will tilt your head back and laugh at the sky".

To attain this bliss requires we arrive at a state of consciousness that embraces all equally. Often people have asked me what true "spiritual love" actually is. What I know is that it is not like the personal love some of us share together. It is truly unconditional, impersonal, and an automatic loving response to all creation, one and all. There is "no taking sides" in this love. We are able to distinguish an ego behavior, but it has no relevance to the whole-hearted love we feel for all beings. We are never against anyone; we are one with everyone.

Now I must offer a few words on a very important aspect of this that has come up before. Many people misunderstand this type of Forgiveness as a feeling that would create passivity in us. Not so!! True Forgiveness allows us to reach a state of calm and openness. Only then are we in a mental position to genuinely and sincerely listen for the guidance as to what actions, if any, are required and to appropriately correct any situation with others or in ourselves.

When do we discipline our children with the greatest wisdom and effectiveness? When we are angry and impulsive or when we have calmed down and thought things through? So this is not a philosophy of passivity in any way. This is a philosophy of acting from a space of wisdom and Divine guidance. Our finest opportunity of impacting all beings and circumstances comes from acting from that inner space of discerning love.

I'd like to share an experience I was privileged to have several years ago that enhanced my ability to Forgive immensely. A powerful personal experience can be worth thousands of hours of study and deliberation and this one was one of those. At that time I intellectually understood what true Forgiveness is and the concepts that underlie its reality. I was making good inroads in implementing it in my everyday life, especially in Forgiving myself, though knowing I had a long way still to go. This wonderful moment really pushed me ahead.

I was working with a client in my private practice. He had experienced a great deal of pain in his life and, in what little we had investigated, had gone through many deeply trying situations in other lives as well. As a result he had developed a disturbing personality. He was very quarrelsome, angry, negative to everything, and extremely hard to like. He came to sessions willingly but was unwilling to truly engage once there. Our work was going very slowly.

My desire to be of some assistance to this person's healing was sincere. I knew that whenever I gave in to any irritation with him, even though I did not show any evidence of this outwardly, it was damaging him further. Remember energy is contagious. We know we can often feel another's emotional state and they ours'. A great deal of our communication takes place unconsciously. He would experience my irritation and impatience at some level. He and I did speak of much of this openly together which was positive but that had not yet had much beneficial impact on the healing work.

As you will understand after you have read the MAP chapter further ahead, I do my work with a uniquely helpful professional MAP Team in addition to my personal MAP Team. These Team members are advanced spiritual beings available to assist us at all times and all ways. And I had sought guidance and requested special assistance from my spiritual buddies in this case.

During one session when he was being particularly objectionable, I felt myself whisked out of present time for a moment and a deeply illuminating vision was before me. First I saw him as he appeared in my office with current body and personality. Then I was shown the deep levels of fear and pain that were beneath the exterior and many scenes of what had created that fear and pain appeared in succession. I had intellectually recognized these aspects of his being but temporarily being present to them occurring had a more powerful impact. I very briefly was literally reliving some of these events.

Then the apex of the experience presented itself which was the most magnificent and beautiful vision of him as his true Self, his Soul. In other words the ultimate reality of who we all are appeared there in all it's glorious array. The beauty, and light, and love were profound. I was definitely being invited to understand and maintain the awareness that, yes, that is most definitely who we all are at the Soul level. He had no knowledge of this experience, however, it was having its designed effect on me. And, interestingly, our work proceeded with much more effectiveness and harmony thereafter. Ah, such blessings!

There really are no adequate words to express the power of that Divine Presence and I shall indeed never forget it. We are invited to begin to heal ourselves and others by not allowing ourselves to drop down in consciousness and think of ourselves as just the body and mind. We are asked to strive wholeheartedly to see the Divinity in us all at all times. Whenever I am able to resurrect that knowledge and experience, everything is transformed and I feel free and light. I am then a being of much greater love and, surely, see things differently.

I had one further experience of that nature some years later with a close personal friend which underlined with great emphasis who we really are. I was meditating at my friend's home while he was asleep in his room. Suddenly he was there in front of me just as he always looked. However, he was not in physical form. He was immensely brilliant, simply radiant with an unbounding love and wisdom. I was overwhelmed.

That experience as well generously illustrated that we are far from who we think we are. Definitely all this is just a temporary drama, life being a seemingly long teachable moment as they say these days. This has changed my perception of everyone and everything to an even greater extent. I am further unburdened and my mind is so much more quiet and gentle. This is all well worth considering, my friends. Your peace and love for yourself and others are extremely important to you and to us all.

The following is a short section of reminders of what we have discussed that consists of a handout that some of our study group members have found useful and suggested that I include here at the end of this chapter. It's a quick reference section that reminds us of many of the concepts we've just gone over and, actually, a few that we haven't. Perhaps you will find it useful as well. I refer to it often.

FORGIVENESS DAILY REMINDERS

Forgiveness releases a great burden from us, whether we are forgiving ourselves or another. Our body, mind, and spirit are all stressed when carrying grievances. Additionally Forgiveness does extend help to the offender as well as the entire world through our healed energies. Forgiveness does not imply allowing ongoing inappropriate behavior, another's or our own. Forgiveness allows us a calmer, gentler heart and mind to make a better decision on appropriate action. The following concepts are worthy of thought to develop wiser, more peaceful reactions to life.

- Our true identity and being is our eternal Divine Soul.
- We are only here, temporarily, on a journey of spiritual growth and awakening.
- All occurrences have meaning and are opportunities for advancement.
- Many events in our lives have been agreed upon by our Soul in its wisdom.
- Other events have wisely or unwisely developed from our own choices and behaviors.
- Karma is a learning tool, not a punishment; God is not angry and vengeful.

- We are only here for further development, not to fulfill our ego's desires.
- We do not know what is best for ourselves or others in terms of spiritual growth.
- Thus, although we surely feel it to be so at times, there are no victims.
- True peace and joy do not depend on outer circumstances, only inner awakening.
- We are never alone in this difficult process; always Divine Beings assist us.

Chapter 6
Creating Loving and
Healed Relationships

The concepts we addressed in the last two chapters can truly revolutionize how we think about our relationships and the feelings and behaviors that we bring into our interactions. How we think about all of life, the purpose and meaning of each day and each interaction, and the lessening of our attachment to all our external circumstances allows relationships to flow much more smoothly and lovingly.

I'll review and apply a few of these concepts from the previous two chapters from some different angles and toss in a few extras. These three chapters work together as a whole. Repetition, as I mentioned several times, is exceptionally helpful to us as we wrestle with more advanced viewpoints.

Although we typically think about relationships as being our connection with other people, it is equally important to evaluate our relationship with ourselves. Are we our own best friend or sometimes our worst enemy? All that we discuss here can be applied to our inner relationship. We likely also realize we have relationships with a huge variety of things. It is enlightening to look at all we have believed will make us whole and contented which, in fact, has not accomplished the task beyond brief spans of time.

Examples of what many of us have placed false faith in are food, drugs, alcohol, work, houses, clothes, promotions, cars, money, sex, others' opinions, shopping, exercise, superficial religious identification, health, how our children are doing, how many electronic toys we play with, and on it goes. I'm sure you can add some of your pets. And then, of course, there are actual pets, typically the four-legged variety. Of course, our central topic – relationships with people – ranks high among the addictions. I'm certainly not saying that some of these things do not have a role to play in our lives; not at all. However our inner peace is much more secure when we do not look to these possessions and activities for our sense of worthiness and completion.

Ken Keyes, many years ago, included in one of his books a discussion of the difference between being addicted to something and having a preference for it. We are beings currently hanging out in human form which means we have desires. We are works in progress. It is terrific when we begin to work our addictions down to simply being preferences. An addiction is when we feel that if that particular thing is not available or does not go our way, we are negatively emotionally affected, perhaps devastated. This adds up to lots of suffering when our addictions are not fulfilled, and lots of conflicts in relationships as well.

Having preferences is rather unavoidable in many situations for most of us, whether those are wise preferences or not. A preference indicates our interest and desire and likely our efforts toward making something happen. However, if it doesn't manifest, it does not affect us deeply. We are not addictively attached to it. We may have come to realize our fulfillment does not come from outer circumstances, from having our way. And we may now understand that we truly don't know what is the best for everyone in any situation. We are more likely to actually feel "Thy Will be done" – a surrendering to Higher Wisdom. We really prefer certain things; but if they don't go our way, we're still cool.

So one of the secrets to successful relationships is working toward living preferentially instead of addictively, which is part of the Buddha's middle path. The Buddha made it beautifully and abundantly clear that desire and attachment are the root of all suffering. The great spiritual teacher, J. Krishnamurti, once said that his great secret to enlightenment was that He didn't mind what happened. I've heard many beautiful variations of that theme of wise detachment from other great teachers. That goes far beyond preferential living and truly illustrates the knowledge that we have no idea what should be happening at any level, at any time, with anyone, for all and anyone's ultimate good. Krishnamurti was at peace with whatever took place.

In this chapter, however, I am focusing on our relationships with people which surely and importantly includes our relationship with ourselves which, in most cases, is definitely in need of enhancement. In the Alice A. Bailey materials, which have been hugely influential in my life for decades, it is stated that troubled personal relationships are one of our greatest gifts. That surely seems in contradiction to most of our beliefs and desires! It emphasizes that close relationships are where most of our conflicts show up and thus give us the maximal opportunity for gaining insight into our issues and working them through.

This invites us back to the concept that we have taken another dip in earth life for the purpose of remembering truth and awakening to Higher Reality. The world teaches us that we are here to have as much pleasure as possible and make our life's circumstances as much to our ego liking as can be. Following that belief system can be a very stressful journey.

Of course it is some effort to awaken to the higher truths of what life is really all about. But what worthy effort that is! It helps us to ask ourselves what we really think relationships are for. What role do they take for the purpose of our life? Most of us unfortunately believe they are to make us feel good, to make us feel complete and have comfortable companionship. Once we have worked through more of our wounds and fears, relationships do feel much better to us.

The Course reminds us that we all carry a significant load of guilt and fear, whether or not it is apparent to us. In my forty-five years of doing psychotherapy that has been validated for me. We might have to dig in some but it is there influencing us even more when it is buried. The Course further suggests that the more out of touch with our issues we are, the more we are going to project negative images onto others. The more we can judge and blame others, the more innocent we can feel and keep our guilt and fear out of sight.

I want to add here that I believe we very often unconsciously choose our close relationships to serve our growth. We hear someone say they repeatedly get involved with the same type of person with the same type of issues again and again. They often judge themselves for that. There are underlying reasons for our choices however.

We have unhealed wounds and issues from our past, this life or another, and without knowing it, we get involved with people who are likely to act in such a way as to open those wounds again. It feels terrible, but it is another chance to take a look at what remains unforgiven in our hearts and minds, what patterns we still cling to, and go further in our insight and healing. To simply blame another for the problem just enlarges the wound even though they may well play a role.

I've worked with a number of couples through the years who have had tremendous difficulty getting along and finding any peace and joy together. When this occurs, most folks these days just split and I won't presume to say that that isn't the appropriate action in some cases. Although I firmly believe that even then to go our separate ways without taking a good look at the process and pattern that has demonstrated itself in our troubles is a real loss. And one person can do that alone even if their partner just won't show up for the growth. It is more difficult but possible.

However, being a transpersonal psychologist has allowed me the privilege to work with many people with more advanced perspectives on life and its struggles. They have seen leaving as not necessarily being the initial answer to deep conflict, at least not without some serious inner evaluation and effort to heal what ails them in the connection.

A humorous interjection here: I can't remember where I first heard this but the example struck me as not only true but it was also funny. I've repeated it in workshops many times. It is acting out a little role play where two or more beings are discussing their upcoming lives together on earth and which roles they will play for greater wisdom and change during that particular lifetime.

They're fussing about which hang-ups they'll take on for that life to help everyone involved to grow. One being says he had to be the bad guy last time and he wants a break from that now. But that leaves the other person to have to take on lousy issues and traits they don't want to carry in this one either. And they fuss and fume to decide which roles they are willing to take on for this particular incarnation. Eventually they come to agreement after remembering what a brief span of time a life is and that it will all change next time. They lighten up. I think the vignette suggests a perspective worth examining.

We are told we often do incarnate in the same group of folks. We most certainly return to unresolved issues. In one of Robin Williams' films, "What Dreams May Come", some cosmic truths are offered us and this relationship issue is one of them. We keep coming back until we get it right, until we awaken out of this vast illusion of life that our ego desires and beliefs have formed. Often we return with the same Souls all making efforts to shake off the false concepts. If you haven't seen that film, it is worth checking out.

So back to the couples who have the wisdom and endurance to use their conflicts to look deeper into themselves, what is not healed and what attachments and expectations are playing a role in their difficulties. Sometimes they work in a psychotherapeutic setting, often they MAP (chapter 26), but always they take quiet time, ask for higher help, and reflect on what they are really feeling inside. Then they go on to examine what belief systems about relationships and themselves are spawning the negative emotions.

And when they do this in light of the spiritual principles that feel right to them, a different perspective often begins to emerge. They look less at the faults of their partner. They tend to believe that they have agreed to or are personally involved in creating the circumstances they are in. They are attempting to believe that everyone involved is doing the best they currently can, given all that is unhealed and unknown in each.

They listen more closely for their own fears resounding in their thoughts and how those fears can influence how they experience everything around them. We may tell ourselves unconsciously "I'm not good enough but I'll see this in you instead and I won't have to deal with it." Or perhaps "If people find out how unworthy I am, I will be alone and lonely", and another common one is "If I am not the first to accuse, anger and accusation may be turned on me." And so it goes until we develop a healthier perspective. Sometimes the thoughts and personal belief systems are buried deeply.

When we are in emotional trouble, a very helpful exercise is to take a sizeable piece of paper, draw a line down through the middle, and on the left side write down every negative thought you hear in your mind related to a particular situation. Then make the effort to become very calm, ask for Divine guidance, and on the right side of the paper, write your more wise and rational thoughts about the situation that may correct what's on the left.

Listen for your inner truth. Perhaps do this multiple times. When you feel you have some thoughts on the right that hold real substance, fold the paper in half and review your truth on the right side each day. See what impact these more advanced perspectives have on you. I usually call the left side the wounded thoughts and the right side the wise thoughts. I and others have often spent months adding to and subtracting from these personal work sheets. It is our responsibility to change the content of our minds.

One of the pieces of wisdom that I am reiterating here that usually impacts relationships quite well is realizing that our happiness does not rely on the other person being a certain way and fulfilling our desires so that we may feel whole and happy. That must come from our own inner healing. Our expectations begin to change and are gentler.

How strange – I'm thinking of President John F. Kennedy right now and his request in the sixties that we not ask ourselves what our country can do for us but rather what we can do for our country. That affected me profoundly at the time. Now it is turned around in my mind so that we might ask not what our relationship can do for us but rather what we can do for our relationship. Only an individual well on the path to inner healing can take that seriously and act on it. However our relationships strongly shift for the better when that occurs. We could choose to make that one of our goals.

This doesn't mean that partners never part. It doesn't mean we permit abusive behavior with ourselves or our children. It does, however, help partners to use the teachings of that relationship as successfully as possible and to more quietly know within where the relationship really needs to go. If couples who have done this work ultimately decide to part, it is usually in a more amicable way.

An exercise that many couples have found advantageous is using the reminder concepts summarized at the end of chapter 5. They independently go down through the lists and mark which principles they presently feel play a role in their life together or could beneficially play a

49

role in the future to ease their conflicts. They take time to really talk together about how they want these ideas to help heal their problems. And healing does begin to come about in many cases.

Again, one person can do this with benefit even if the other individual is not interested. We can absolutely apply these just ourselves alone and bring about much less conflict and much greater satisfaction. All these concepts apply equally to any relationship or connection - with our children, friends, co-workers or anyone. Our change of perspective and resulting behaviors are very powerful in our environment. We can take the high road first and mark the trail.

I highly value Eckhart Tolle's work on our pain bodies. He is hugely helpful in our seeing things differently and staying in the moment. We all have sizable pain bodies developed from many sources as we've considered before and bringing awareness to that in the moment gives us a great opportunity to work with that pain and bring healing to what ails us. Just bringing the space of our breath awareness to any situation allows for less identification with our wounded reactions and increases our ability to choose our response more wisely.

Tolle's suggestion to live in the Now helps us to drop back into witnessing our troubled emotions and thoughts rather than thinking we are them. If you haven't read Tolle's *The Power of Now* and *A New Earth*, please consider doing so. They are very powerful. What a great difference all this can make. We truly are not victims. We can begin to take charge of our perceptions of ourselves and others, uplevel them, and our thoughts and emotions will soon reflect that enhanced understanding. There is where the true happiness and peace lie.

A personal example here: a couple of decades back my husband and I purchased a property we wanted to develop organically. I was still working more than full time and was in my late forties. There was so much work to do. And I thought I was in better shape than I was. So in no time at all I had injured my knee and that injury kept me from exercising and working on our home area.

I went to physical therapy, that helped some and I MAPed on the injury and that also assisted. But it still continued to plague me and kept me from many physical activities. I was working diligently on communicating with my MAP Team at that time and they shared with me that they chose not to heal it further because unconsciously I wanted to maintain the injury. They said that I needed an excuse to not take on all this extra home work when I was already very busy and I used the knee injury to my advantage.

They further shared that I needed to work on my passivity in telling my husband I just couldn't do all that was needed and about my fear of his disapproval. They added that I was angry at him, unnecessarily, because I had never asked for what I really needed. My fears were very much in the way of a more open relationship with my spouse and were interfering with my healing. So I got busy and worked on all of that with fairly good success and then the knee healed.

Obviously, this is just one example of how our unconscious fears can bring about inadequate behavior in us and put blame on the other person. My husband was completely cooperative when I fully explained my feelings and needs. We so often don't know our deeper levels of emotions and, even when we do, we usually do not communicate those effectively, if at all. We can make new choices on that with determination.

Well, I'm hopeful there have been some thoughts here that may be beneficial to some of you. We attend many years of education and yet have so little training in the basic emotional needs of life, of communication, and of those deeper levels of ourselves. It is encouraging that many school systems have begun to incorporate these basic life skills in their curriculums and I hope many more will do so. These concepts can take us forward in important areas and lead to better relationships, improved self-esteem, the big-picture viewpoints and enhanced health. They are a win all the way around.

A quote that stirs me deeply is by our great spiritual teacher of the twentieth century, Thich Nhat Hanh. It is in a piece he wrote in 1987 entitled "Being Peace". He states "Reconciliation is to understand both sides; to go to one side and describe the suffering being endured by the other side; then go to the other side and describe the suffering being endured by the first side."

This exercise in wisdom, in any situation - whether it be a personal relationship or a great confrontation in the world - uplevels our perspective immensely. Accomplished with a true grasp of higher realities, it has the potential to heal the world. It is, in part, another way of stating that we must learn to walk in each other's shoes. Our walk will be much lighter if we have understanding and compassion for all including ourselves. Relationships will be filled with harmony and love.

We now have two heart-warming testimonies coming up in the next chapter offered to us by two of our long-term *A Course in Miracles* students. These are some very fine words of wisdom forged through years of study and practice. I thank them both heartily.

Chapter 7
Testimonies to A Course in Miracles

A LIFE CHANGED
by Leslie Underdonk, M.A.

A Course in Miracles has radically changed my life and has taught me to see from a different perspective. I was raised in the Methodist Church. One day I found myself thinking about Solomon. He could have anything he desired and the one thing he asked for was wisdom. So I decided that that was what I would ask for as well. I was sincere in my asking and hoped for a response, but what I received was totally not what I expected. What I received was *A Course in Miracles*.

I saw it on my sister's coffee table and was quickly drawn to it because of the title. What really piqued my interest, though, was the introduction which said, "This is a required course. Only the time you take it is voluntary. Free will does not mean that you can establish the curriculum. It means only that you can elect what you want to take at a given time..." Surprisingly, my sister was not a student of the Course so she gave me her copy of the book.

I started reading the text on my own. I had no one to talk with about it, and I didn't understand half of what I was reading; but I knew that I held the "truth" in my hands and that my request for wisdom had been answered. A couple of years later after I had finished the text, I was led through prayer to my Course discussion group. It was so inspiring and uplifting to finally get to talk with other students about the Course. I also loved that one of the members of the group said that this was "one" spiritual path. The Course didn't claim to be "the only game in town" and that it had the exclusive inside track.

The Course is with me all the time. I start each day reading it and saying a prayer from the Course that has strengthened me:

"I am here only to be truly helpful.
I am here to represent Him Who sent me.
I do not have to worry about what to say or what
to do, because He Who sent me will direct me.
I am content to be wherever He wishes, knowing
He goes there with me.
I will be healed as I let Him teach me to heal."

I now realize that we are on a spiritual journey and the only goal we need to work on is getting out of the ego belief system that we have adopted. I know that we have great help at any given moment and constantly need to seek for higher guidance. The Course has made me see how truly crazy my thoughts can be. It has made me realize that we are responsible for our lives and what we choose to see. "Choose again" is a phrase I hold on to when I know I'm caught in a negative ego moment. "This need not be" reminds me that I have chosen to look at something through my lower mind. I can choose to see things in a different way. "I am responsible for what I see." As I work with these Course quotes, my love and peace and joy in life accelerate and I am grateful.

The secret of salvation is that we are doing this to ourselves but we can also undo it. We are part of God but have gotten lost in our ego. The Course is helping us to remember who we really are. The main lesson to learn is to forgive everyone everything, but the Course teaches us that it is not forgiveness as the world knows it. This forgiveness is different because this forgiveness is unconditional and based on our wisdom of how this world works and who we truly are.

This is probably one of the hardest ideas to grasp. That's where the Workbook has been invaluable. Unconditional forgiveness is such a hard idea that we need to practice every day and take one step at a time in changing our perspective. The lessons in the workbook are taught over and over, are reinforced and are extremely necessary for a change in perspective. The Course has transformed my life and every day is a new adventure with a new revelation being conveyed. I am so grateful to have found these amazing words from Jesus.

FINDING PEACE
By John N. Kramer, DDS

It was the fall of 1994 and I had walked out of a house that was just completed after a five-year project and a marriage of seven years. I told myself it was so I could get away from "everything" for a short period of time, a breather so to speak. I needed to get my head right.

I had no peace, not that I really understood what "peace" meant. I could not sleep. To eat was a chore. I hadn't been able to get far enough away from my wife in bed. I exercised to exhaust myself in hopes that my self-induced exercise pain would somehow relieve my inner pain. I went to work to distract my mind from the whirling thoughts of guilt and condemnation. I had hundreds of friends and patients, yet I felt all alone. I knew that there had to be a better way of living than what I was doing. Certainly, I said to myself, life had to be better than this.

Bill called me about a week after I had walked out. Not that we were best of friends, but rather a friend who had heard I was going through a tough time. He invited me to attend a workshop he was hosting in West Virginia the following weekend and it was titled "A Psychological Spiritual Retreat for the Soul". Enter Miracle number 1. I knew I had to go.

The workshop was built around Marianne Williamson's bestselling book, *A Return to Love*, which is based on *A Course in Miracles*. The weekend changed my life. For the first time, I heard about and started to consider that life was a journey, that there are no accidents in this life and that all events can and should be used for our personal growth. I heard about love vs. the ego. I was told about forgiveness of self, since we were all doing the best we can. I felt I was accepted in spite of what I felt about myself. Had I found a better way?

The answer has been a resounding YES to the last question and I have been working with the Course since that weekend in West Virginia eighteen years ago.

Here are some of the changes I have felt:

1. There is much more peace in my life and I am slowly and surely grasping what "the peace of God" means.
2. I feel hope. Hope that with a new relationship with Jesus (God/Higher Self...use your word) my life can have joy; that heartache does not dominate my existence.
3. I am choosing love more often than fear, and that makes me feel good.
4. Forgiveness has taken on a new meaning for me, and that has made all the difference.
5. I am experiencing that I am not alone. That Jesus is by my side at all times and in all ways, nurturing, calming and helping me along my journey.

Rest assured that the journey has not always been easy, but by studying, listening and applying ACIM to my daily life, my journey has been much better. As the Course says, "there are thousands of paths Home". May this book point you in your direction.

Chapter 8
Our Spiritual Journey
thru the Master's Eyes

*A*nother series of works that has been invaluable to me for almost forty years are the Ancient Wisdom Teachings as they are traditionally called. I'll outline only a few of the major concepts since there are over twenty books in this entire Bailey series. It will give you a taste. They were dictated to Alice A. Bailey from 1919 to 1949 by the Tibetan Master Djwahl Khul, more commonly spoken of as The Tibetan or DK. It conveys once again some of the principles that we have already considered. However, as you can imagine, in twenty-six books a great many more spiritual truths are offered for our consideration.

We are indeed on a magnificent journey as an eternal Divine Spirit. We have a degree of free will in the journey but to do the journey is non-negotiable. We begin as a Soul, the Higher Self. The Soul is part of God and remains in union with the Divine during the journey. If we are one with God and made of love in the beginning, what's the purpose of making the journey at all? Many do ask this reasonable question.

One way of talking about the purpose of our pilgrimage is to use the analogy of innocent faith versus tried faith. A person might begin with faith in God and His love but has not yet been through hardship. As the years go by we endure many types of pain and crises. Our faith may be sorely tried and tested. We will develop in strength, love, courage, compassion, and forgiveness as we open to the lessons our difficulties offer. A being of this tried faith is more stable and more knowing by far than one untried. Our journey of millions of years produces eventually a being far more advanced and capable. We will have been made strong and wise and enduring through the fire of experience. We are being trained for ever more mighty roles and tasks as the eons roll by.

Thus there is much evolution of the Soul taking place through the vast expanse of time. Physical bodies are our temporary vehicles during part of our journey. These physical bodies have been of many varieties representing the mineral, plant, animal, and human kingdoms in times past. That is the evolution of the physical body, the Darwinian process. The Soul is only housed by the human physical body. Its evolution is not Darwinian. People confuse this often. We are the Soul in our own evolutionary pattern and temporarily inhabit physical bodies which have been in a different evolutionary pattern. The human physical bodies on this planet had to mature to a certain level before they became useful to the expression of our Souls.

We are now working toward moving into the next kingdom, the spiritual kingdom, where physical bodies are no longer needed but continued learning abounds. We have vast and great adventures ahead as our spiritual evolution goes on through time beyond our comprehension. Continued evolution does not entail continued pain and strife such as we know now, be assured.

As we move through this measureless educational curriculum, we clearly do reincarnate innumerable times. Our Souls continue our expansion of consciousness in and out of physical bodies. There is no such event as death. We simply release from the physical vehicle and shift our focus to a higher form of ourselves. As has been said by the great teacher Emmanuel channeled by Pat Rodegast "death is like taking off a tight shoe; it is a totally safe process". We do not regress and take an animal form again; we are consistently moving forward. How quickly is up to us. Again at some point in our awakening we will not require a physical form at all; our evolution will continue in our spiritual being. We will then be residing in the spiritual kingdom.

The principle that governs our progress and experience in the human body is that of karma, cause and effect. What goes around does come around. "Do unto others as you would have them do unto you." Every religion offers some form of this teaching reminding us that we do sow what we reap. Not only our actions, but every thought, feeling, and word are energies that influence ourselves and others and have karmic repercussions.

Our goal is to become wise, loving, and selfless beings; to remember the wisdom that has always been tucked away inside our consciousness. To experience the natural consequences of our inner and outer actions gradually takes us in this direction. There is not only personal karma to experience and learn from but also family, group, nation, and general human karma offered us as part of our learning experience. Thus, many of us have come to recognize there truly are no accidents. Every single occurrence of our lives has meaning and opportunity and is offered to us by the universe in love. Karma must be balanced and our learning must proceed. Remember it is not a punishment but rather a road to awakening.

Nonetheless, many of us have often said "I want to be done with this reincarnation process ASAP. It hurts and I'm tired." This is a mighty tough curriculum to be sure. But our Divine Source did not design it as such. The Master DK tells us that long, long ago we committed what is often called "the ancient error". We know little about it specifically. The Christian Bible represents the event with the Adam and Eve metaphor. We are told it involved "premature compassion" of some nature. It was a serious wrong turn in humanity's development, one we chose in free will but not wisdom, and moving past the consequences of that error has involved a great deal of suffering.

We would do well to remember that God has not tossed us into an agonizing process and is not punishing us for our error. Our difficult journey is a result of our own wrong choosing of the past and present. A common word used in these writings is "personality" which very generally refers to the lower self's totality of thoughts, feelings, belief systems, unhealed wounds, and ways we interface with the world. It is what we usually think of as ourselves which, of course, is woefully inadequate. It is only this, our personality, which suffers; our Soul remains in peace and bliss with God. Our task and what this book is about is to uplevel all these aspects of ourselves to reach our true Soul union, serenity and love.

Karma is very much misunderstood. We talk of good and bad karma. That is from the perspective of humans who like to have things our way; we like to be comfortable. True, there is karma that is easier and karma that is more difficult. There are karmic occurrences that are pleasant and those that are challenging. But all those judgments come from our lower self's value system. We really do think we know what is best for ourselves and others. Our limited perspective doesn't allow for that expanded wisdom. We've entertained that concept in several different chapters and it is so worthwhile contemplating once again. Its potential for our peace of mind is vast.

Karma, in any variety, is a gift to us to take us past our suffering. On my computer's screen saver I have placed the opening line from a writing of a Fourth Century Chinese Patriarch stating "The Great Way is not difficult for those who know no preferences". We are here to go beyond preferences. This may remind us of Khrishnamurti's statement that he doesn't mind what happens. We are here to invariably surrender to the sentiment "Not my will but Thine, O Lord". Preferences shrink as our vision expands.

We are invited to go beyond karma as soon as possible. Our goal is to rise to such a state of consciousness that we are completely guided by harmlessness and loving compassion for all. When that day arrives, we move beyond human karma. We are free; free to continue our journey much less encumbered.

Toward the end of the human journey, we go through five spiritual initiations signifying certain developmental attainments. Our curriculum requires we gradually gain greater control of our entire being and release our personality attachments. This produces what is similar to what Gary Zukav calls a multi-sensory being. His material on this is excellent. The following is a brief summary of these initiations.

Our first initiation signifies a good measure of control over the excessive appetites of the physical body. We are less impulsive and more guided by wisdom in these appetites.

Our second initiation signifies that same level of control over our emotions and emotional or astral body. We certainly have emotions but they do not rule our behavior in general.

Our third initiation signifies control over our mental body, our thoughts. We have now attained alignment with our Soul thus permitting much more profound responses to life.

Our fourth initiation is entitled the "great renunciation" at which time we have released all human attachments and are no longer required to reincarnate in human form.

Our fifth initiation entitled "the resurrection" signifies our attainment of the elevated state of the Masters with all the authority, wisdom, freedom, and responsibility of that state then being ours.

These descriptions obviously bring up the question of our various bodies beyond the physical. Many of us are aware of our energy field surrounding our physical bodies; many call them auras. They are quite complex. The Bailey material delineates our various bodies as the etheric, astral (emotional), mental (thoughts), and causal (surrounding our Souls). Each extends throughout our physical selves and beyond. And every thought, word, emotion, and deed affects each of these parts of us for better or worse. We are vast beings of energy. Our chakras, or energy vortexes, exist in this field. The Master DK offers us excellent material on these parts of ourselves and our chakra system.

We are not alone and without assistance and solace during any part of this journey. There are a variety of loving beings present and available in this system to guide and support us along the way as we discuss in our next chapter in detail. We are all equal in our potential and our ultimate being. However, there are many beings ahead of and behind us on this adventure through time. That is our good fortune since it allows us excellent company and counsel from those more advanced, especially from all members of our Spiritual Hierarchy.

The Spiritual Hierarchy guides the happenings of this planet. The concept is similar to the "family of saints" sometimes referred to in Christianity. They are beings who have completed the human part of the journey and choose to remain connected to this planet to help us in our efforts to awaken. The Hierarchy, often called the Masters of Wisdom, are governed and directed by our World Teacher, sometimes known as the Christ as well as many other names of resplendence known throughout the traditions of the world.

The true Christ is not a Being simply connected to Christians but is a loving Father to all on this planet. He loves and guides peoples of all religions and of none. The World Teacher and the Masters are, in truth, beyond gender as certainly is God. We use such pronouns as convenience only. The Masters and initiates and disciples of the Light (including ourselves) work under the World Teacher's great tutelage and inspiration to heal and awaken everyone on Mother Earth and to heal Mother Earth herself.

Here I would like to insert a beautifully descriptive section about the Masters from a book entitled *Dialogues With The Holy Spirit*, a truly inspirational and uplifting work. It was published in 2011 by my dear friend and mentor, Dr. Rusty Stephens. It adds a further dimension to our understanding of the Spiritual Hierarchy and Rusty has graciously allowed his material to be included in this book.

> Masters too are evolving. Their evolution is just as much a part of the Plan as your own. By Their service Masters are growing in Their own wisdom and capacity to see ever greater parts of the Plan and to render that vision into practical manifestation.

> At the head of Earth's group of Masters is the great Lord, the One They all look to for wise counsel and loving leadership. He in turn consults Them on Their various aspects of world governance and draws upon the wisdom of the group for His direction. He also receives support and guidance from Those with greater vision and more highly evolved capacities than His own. While it

may be difficult for us to imagine Beings more highly evolved than Masters, there are. These Beings are Themselves lesser to greater Ones than They. The aggregation of this great chain of Being is one way to think of God.

Masters then represent your connection to the higher and are working to bring about a greater understanding of the Universe and its working out to mankind. Indeed it will be this knowledge interpreted through Their wisdom which will inform and initialize the next great unfoldment. It is underway now and has been for some time. It cannot be stopped. However, once the significance of this is understood by man, he will want to embrace it. He will rush to embrace it for not only is it his salvation, it will be his joy, his bliss, and his new life.

I find these paragraphs very uplifting. Rusty's entire book is one of deep inspiration.

Now we go to the important purpose of temptation and suffering in our spiritual progress. These are like barbells for our spiritual strengthening. They bring about Soul and personality exercise and vigor. There are dark forces in the universe and connected to our earth evolution although not of the satanic model so many believe in. They are typically disembodied humans who are lost in lower self desires and form a significant number of these tempters although there are other forms as well.

There are various forms of what most people call "evil" in the world and beyond. More enlightened individuals think of evil as unknowing energies and entities having a state of unconsciousness that is unaware as yet of the Higher Realities and God's ever abiding love for us all. That will change for them at some point, do not fear. We are only vulnerable to temptation and darkness when we are in our own state of lower self desires and emotions, dwelling in our own misunderstanding of who we really are. Dealing with temptation makes us ultimately much stronger. Always ask for that higher help that is forever present. Of course many temptations arise simply from our own ego desires. In fact, the vast majority of them do.

Suffering only occurs as a result of our clinging to having things be the way we wish or think that they should. That even includes a great portion of physical suffering which intensifies with our resistance to what is at the moment, physically or otherwise. Again suffering is not of God's will or design but a result of our losing our way on the path forward. The Buddha's teachings centered on the passage out of suffering. He helped us to see that all suffering is based in personal desire, wanting things to be a certain way. Releasing our desires immediately decreases anguish. A wise being hears the subtle whisper of needed change and heeds the call - no agony required.

A terrific Bailey book to begin with is *Initiation Human and Solar*. It is not a large book and is an excellent piece of material in which to test the Bailey waters. There are other authors who have written some fine materials more gently introducing us to these great teachings. An excellent international lecturer on the Wisdom Teachings, William Meader, has written a book that is a great treasure entitled *Shine Forth: The Soul's Magical Destiny*. It can be secured through www.meader.org.

I have barely touched the surface here of this magnificent revelation. In these twenty-six books are quite varied topics including esoteric healing, Soul astrology, white magic, the reappearance of the Masters and the World Teacher, the rays and initiations, esoteric psychology, discipleship in the New Age and much more. I have never come across a finer array of higher teachings and they have proved themselves to me by their products in my life over and over again. By all means, consider doing a spiritual taste test.

Chapter 9
Our Heavenly Helpers

*T*here truly is a tremendous amount of wise and advanced assistance and guidance available to us all. We know these are very important and difficult times. We are at an extremely challenging decision point in the history of planet earth. We are experiencing chaos and much is at stake, for the planet and for ourselves. Thus, guidance and support have become even more important.

The ongoing and powerfully driven energy and assistance that is flowing into us is, in part, directed to the planet as a whole, working with the environment and the earth itself. Yet a great deal of higher guidance and help is always available to us as individuals as well and always has been. Often assistance will come to us in ways we never would have imagined.

Let us very briefly review some of the central players among our heavenly helpers. Our very own Higher Self, our Soul, that deep inner wisdom and holiness that lies within us all is always a good starting place for seeking assistance. We will not complete our journey as a human being until we have completely unified with our Soul. In meditation we begin to solidify that alignment and the guidance from that Source. Likewise this takes place in MAPing and prayer and in other ways as well. Our Soul is always close at hand to guide our path. Its embrace is never further away than our request.

As we have discussed there is a vast union of advanced Souls known often as the Spiritual Hierarchy. These Masters of Wisdom exist at various levels of enlightenment and are continuing Their spiritual journey in part by serving our needs. If there is a particular saint or advanced being that you have read about or beseeched, they are often a member of the Hierarchy and available to our call.

Many of us feel connected to Angels or Devas, as they are often titled, and indeed we are told that there are some angels whose task is to assist humans in our journey. They are involved in many other tasks as well. Nature Spirits are very real also and part of the devic kingdom and work endlessly with components of the natural world for everyone's betterment. A few of my friends, who have trained in energy work, are able to see these wondrous beings and find great solace with them.

That's one of the reasons I rave on about the many benefits of regular and continued MAPing because that process quite scientifically brings together appropriate members of all of the above types of beings for our healing and betterment. *MAP*, 3rd edition by Machaelle Small Wright, is a terrific eye-opening read; give it a try! And, of course, chapter 26 on MAP lies ahead.

Many of us also feel very connected to beings we call Guides. In my experience, this is a name used to cover an array of helpful beings. Often we feel various types of support coming our way and aren't really certain what the source is. However, we could receive help from any of the beings mentioned in this material and feel them to be Guides. They all are in the general sense of the word. Our task is to choose what beings most cultivate our highest awareness and which feel most comfortable to us. We don't need to specifically direct a prayer actually; we simply call out in sincerity and openness. It is completely our choice.

Again, I must mention that our inner discernment is very important in all of this in two ways. First, if we do wish to specifically direct a request, who we are at peace connecting with must be determined within us as we listen quietly for our own truth. Secondly, there are some beings who wish to help us but don't really have sufficient wisdom to guide us well. Just because a human is finished with a particular incarnation doesn't mean they automatically become all knowing to say the least.

So Uncle Harry may be offering his best but simply doesn't have the knowledge of our whole picture. And, too, there are some beings out there who are most pleased to lead us in false directions. So it is wisest to choose the highest and best source of love and support that we feel comfortable with and stick with that in our quiet moments of seeking. My MAP Team has become that for me each and every day which is not to say that I don't chat up a few other wondrous beings now and again.

Now we come to a tricky one. Some of us are very comfortable with this reality, and indeed very grateful, and some of us are not. We have Space Brothers; there are extraterrestrials who work tirelessly on our behalf to keep our planet up and running as much as possible while we evolve to the wisdom needed to make less environmental mistakes and do more of the clean-up work ourselves. They are very much our brothers. Much of their work is with the planet as a whole but sometimes they work with us as individuals. I personally have been guided and supported many times by my Space Brothers and am immensely appreciative.

Now you may be thinking "I'm not hearing anything about God yet? Where's God in this?" Well, I do tread lightly here. No doubt we are beloved by God. However, many of us have been reared with wrongful and frightening ideas and images about God, even though we may think we have left them behind. When I am privileged to dig deeply inside of someone's mind as they traverse their path, fear of God is almost always found remaining to some extent. So if praying directly to God feels like it works for you, go for it. However, many people today have questions as to who God is and what is His/Her nature and purpose.

So many of us have hidden fears, guilt, and a sense of unworthiness that affects our relationship with our Divine Source so we must be mindful of our true reactions and emotions if we pray to God. Unconditional love is truly the nature of Higher Reality, of God, but many of us simply can't feel that and allow it to be truly accepted within. Pay close attention to your feelings if you pray to God and be willing to notice if you have hesitancies and fears in this connection. If so, either work those through since they are not valid or choose another Divine Being to converse with.

A Course in Miracles frequently urges us to ask for help with whatever challenges arise. I recall years ago one of our Course study members having difficulty asking for guidance. He felt that God was asking that all of us become whole spiritual beings who required no "outside" direction. His hesitancies even extended to asking his own Soul for input.

Several years went by before his serious studies led him to understand that when reaching for that greater wisdom, we are actually aligning with our true Selves. His ideas about not being separate from his Soul, or Higher Self, or God for that matter became wiser. He realized that at that higher level, we are all one. There is no separation. The lower self he was depending upon only had "ego" answers for him. His requests for more advanced assistance were now comfortable for him and provided much finer results thereafter.

When we reach for that deep inner wisdom, we are contacting our true Selves. The Course usually uses the term "Holy Spirit" as who we might all call upon for help. Many feel very comfortable with that title and contact and have had excellent results. Some of us have old wounds connected to the term and need to choose otherwise due to our own emotional response. However, it doesn't matter who we call upon as long as we keep our request genuine. It is all the same wisdom and love.

And now there is "US"! This is an uplifting and inspiring arena for thought. The statistics on the increasing numbers of individuals who give of their love, time and money to help others in a great many ways is wonderfully uplifting. We are all asked to search our Souls for what service to others is right for us. In some literature, we are titled "the new group of world servers". Our role is crucial in transforming the status of this world.

Yet some of the more advanced teachings and my personal experience validates the reality that once we have reached a certain point in our spiritual development, we spend most of our sleeping time in "out-of-body" states, with much of that time being filled with wonderful learning experiences. And a good bit of that education is derived from being guided to assist others in need who do not yet have the wisdom we have garnered. We are heavenly helpers as well.

I have had some awe inspiring experiences doing this; simply wonderful moments of assisting others or joining with other spiritual aspirants to further learn greater truth during the night. Much of this feels vividly real to me. You likely have had some of those moments as well. This doesn't mean that we don't still have normal dreams and that everything we recall from our sleep is to be taken for granted as accurate and pondered deeply however. There are many forms of "sleep" experiences and whatever we recall is most likely filtered through the awareness of our ego mind. So remembering dreams or nighttime experiences accurately is quite complicated.

To stretch our minds a little more, I will claim that even during waking hours, we are active in other dimensions in learning and service capacities. I first encountered that concept in the Seth materials by Jane Roberts in the 70s. Not until somewhere in the 90s did my personal veil thin sufficiently on brief occasions for me to know the validity of this teaching.

I vividly recall the first time I became aware of some aspect of myself being active in a totally separate dimension. I was teaching one of my college classes and speaking at the time. For some reason I suddenly felt completely aware of myself being elsewhere carrying out entirely different activities. For a few seconds, I stood there in shock and then rallied myself to continue my earthly work of the moment so as to not appear too crazy. However, since that event, that type of experience has appeared on a number of occasions, spontaneously or during meditation or MAPing. It is unnerving until we become comfortable with the concept that who we are is much more than what we have supposed.

One other occasion comes to mind right now that became a very educating moment for me. I was reading and suddenly became aware of myself in a very different environment in the midst of an effort to be helpful with a problem in that dimension. However, I didn't remember to stay detached and calm in witnessing this scene and therefore quickly slipped right back into my current earth reality. That quiet detachment is usually crucial to continued awareness in any other state of being.

Then without really thinking things through, I felt concern that what I was doing in that other dimension wasn't being completed and proper help was not being given. I asked my MAP Team to clarify for me if they would and was quickly advised that my witnessing such an occurrence had nothing to do with it being accomplished. Just because I was no longer seeing what was going on in that dimension didn't mean it wasn't continued as designed. It wasn't the "me" of this writing that was carrying out the activity; I was merely temporarily witnessing and observing. Well, of course, that immediately made perfect sense to me; it became a very educational moment.

At this point I wonder if you may be thinking I am lost in demented illusion. I would not try to convince anyone of any experience or belief that I hold to be true. We are always wise to access our own inner spiritual discernment for what is helpful to us at any particular time. I have had many doubts myself at times and sought guidance to know if I was deluding myself. The experiences mentioned herein have, however, been real and useful to me. They have helped me to evolve further along my path and expanded my awareness and love for myself and others.

Something that has furthered my belief in my experiences has been the various times when I witnessed myself doing something at a distance with someone I knew personally whether this be during the night or day. Occasionally they have later contacted me telling me they were aware I was with them and exactly what we did and discussed which matched my own recall. That has been validating. We are truly multi-dimensional and multi-sensory beings. We, too, are members of the Spiritual Hierarchy, albeit junior members in training by and large.

With this vast array of beings to aid us and our own involvement in this work, we might ask why we so often feel alone. It's never true. We might examine our doubts, fears, control issues, and lack of effort to connect and listen to learn more of what blocks our experience. We have such definite ideas about how help arrives and what its nature will be that we often block the path. And, too, so many of us feel unworthy of Divine assistance. Also, many folks have told me that they fear asking for higher guidance as they feel rather certain they won't like the answers; they won't be to their ego liking. Could be! Sometimes it involves deep insight and personal healing to actually be ready to align with higher wisdom.

I have had that dilemma. I had become aware that I feared the answer to my questions at times. For years I had to reconcile that by stating clearly to my Guides that I would do my best to follow any Divine Guidance offered, but that I could not guarantee I would come up with the courage to follow that guidance at all times. By giving myself that out, I was able to be calmer about listening for the inner wisdom. If I had threatened myself with absolute compliance, I know I would have been in the way of much offered wisdom. My Teachers have been quite understanding of this agreement.

How might we improve our access route to higher guidance? Well, we must start by learning to calm ourselves and release our belief that we know how things should be. We must attempt to cast aside any feelings of unworthiness for higher attention. As always meditation is immensely useful; it is often described as listening to God in opposition to prayer, which is talking to God. So learn to listen for an inner feeling or some happening that gives you direction.

I usually tell people to reach for that deepest space of calm and connection that they can attain, state their question and concern with clarity, and very peacefully and simply be aware of what comes to them. Often that is the best that any of us can do. Does that guarantee us fine results? Often, yes; but, not always. However, it assuredly increases our ability to access that higher wisdom and very often the needed guidance is ours. This ability is definitely a work in progress for us all.

And to again sing the praises of the *MAP* book, even if you have no interest in MAPing as a healing process, the chapter on kinesiology in that book focuses on how you can establish two-way communication with those more knowing Beings. Some modes of modern medicine use this method for medical purposes. It is wise to have the book for that reason alone. Some of my friends use pendulums. Whatever we choose as our route, we must maintain purity of mind and desire and every bit of detachment we can muster. We will review some of this material in our "Seeking Divine Guidance" Chapter 30.

As a little afterthought on this Heavenly Helpers topic, I will add for you animal lovers an area of assistance which many people have really felt connected to. I am not entirely sure how all of this takes place, but clearly we often receive help from our beloved animal friends. We all know of stories of animals being loving companions and even saving lives. What great buddies they can be.

However, I think it can go deeper than that. I'll give you an example that feels quite real to me. Some years ago, my husband was very close to one of our cats, Bushy. Bushy followed him everywhere and slept with him at night. Bushy would dig down under the covers and then turn around and stick his head up. He looked just like a furry little person in there. It was uplifting to observe them.

Then Bushy developed feline leukemia and eventually passed on from that disease. What a great loss we felt that to be. Animals, too, have souls; they too go on to other experiences after they have left our company. That is a help to our hearts. Not too many hours after Bushy left his body, he appeared to me very clearly. He telepathically showed me that he had three dark spots in his chest that needed to be removed before he could complete this particular earthly journey.

I asked for higher assistance and began to bring in a healing light to remove these impediments, but Bushy quickly informed me that my husband, Herschel, had to be part of the cleansing process. So I told Herschel of the situation and asked him to join in and, indeed, we did psychically remove those three dark spots and Bushy joyfully moved on to other dimensions.

Now for the next development in this saga. Several years later, Hersch became quite ill and off we went for medical attention. He was subjected to many tests as they had great difficulty reducing his symptoms and diagnosing the problem. They really never did come to a final diagnosis but he gradually improved over a period of time with the help of his MAP Team.

However, as a result of all these tests, it was discovered that Hersch had three dark spots in his lung and the physicians followed those very closely for many months trying to determine what was going on. Finally as a result of lack of activity in these nodules, the physicians concluded that these were three old tumors that had already atrophied. No reason for concern. The years passing since then seem to have validated their conclusion.

My higher guidance on this made it clear that Bushy had, in his love, taken the illness represented by those tumors as a gift to his beloved friend. Those were his three spots we had to cleanse away when he left his body. I don't know if there is a dimension of animal intelligence that makes such a choice or whether higher beings use animals in a positive way to help us humans. I really don't know how it all works. However, some others have told me stories somewhat like this from their own animal experiences.

The animal assistance may be true for me as well. In the late 70s and early 80s I had a cancerous condition. In the early 80s four cats came to live with me and three of the four lived to be 18, 19, and 20 years of age before moving on to other experiences. We had wonderful and warm relationships. Each of these cats died of various cancerous conditions. But I myself became free of it in the mid-80s upon their arrival never to have it resurface again. Interesting! Definitely worth pondering. The mysteries of the universe abound.

Most of us have our own stories of divine assistance and intercession. Also there are many writings these days that describe such interventions. They always bring tears to my eyes. It is so important that we remember to ask for help when needed. It is also very important that we work to prepare ourselves to receive what is offered without any sense of unworthiness and doubt and judgment as to just how it should be. It is true daily effort on our part but we can gradually arrive at that purely receptive inner space. This is an extremely worthy goal, my friends.

Chapter 10
A Profound Experience with Jesus

*Y*ou and I have a deal. I get to write about what is real to and treasured by me with no expectations of you. That gives you the freedom to ignore anything you wish and utilize anything that is helpful. That's our deal. That's very important for this chapter because what I wish to share might be a stretch for some of you. Of course many of you likely have wonderful experiences to relate as well.

So speaking of Heavenly Helpers, as we have been in our last chapter, I will share with you something that happened over twenty years ago and has had a profound influence on my life. It continues to be a daily guiding force.

One afternoon I carried my shopping list into a small local office supply store. A rather forlorn and dejected looking salesperson assisted me. I silently offered him love as it was so apparent that he was in need.

Ultimately we arrived at the cash register and as he completed my credit card transaction, I felt a shift in the energy in the room. I looked up and, lo and behold, there was Jesus superimposed on my forlorn brother. Jesus was radiant! Tears are in my eyes now as I write this. He looked straight at me and in a voice I will never forget said "Here, I want you to have this". This was a very nice black ink pen, at a concrete level, handed to me by the salesperson; however "this" was a lesson of so much more in reality. Seconds later He disappeared with the salesperson being none the wiser.

If the idea of an apparition such as this taking place doesn't seem plausible to you, let me share that there are some fine materials available speaking of such wondrous and healing phenomena. One that comes to mind is Dr. G. Scott Sparrows' book entitled *I Am With You Always: True Stories of Encounters with Jesus*. It is a very worthy read that can open our minds to such great occurrences and offers us such solace.

What I perceived, what I felt, and what I knew in that moment was something of the nature of Jesus' Being. Three Divine qualities were overwhelmingly apparent. He was a Being of such Love that using that word is totally inadequate. That Divine Love so far surpasses anything that we normally exchange here together as humans. It was a rapturous energy encompassing my whole being.

The second quality that flowed right into me was a very deep Peace. It was a steadfast calm and serenity that felt to be firm in all circumstances and grounded in the knowing of the Divine universal realities. And it was highly contagious in that moment as well.

The third quality was even more palpable perhaps because I was so lacking in it myself. He was Joyful, truly bliss-filled. I could feel His joy in doing exactly what He was doing in that moment – blessing and teaching me. And I fully and instinctively knew that Jesus felt that same joy in every task He executed and invited me to do the same. I stumbled out of the store and sat in my car in a daze, asking for help in taking in all that I was meant to from this magnificently rich experience. All of this may have been a tad easier for me to work with because I am a student of *A Course in Miracles* among other works.

In the Course Jesus asks us to consider Him our Elder Brother, One who has traveled our path and gone far beyond. He knows what lies ahead for us and what we must do to traverse the path well. He invites us to rely on Him and seek His advice and guidance which I did and do. In my thinking of Him in this way, this experience was a little easier to embrace.

This moment was of course a great blessing. However it was much more than that. Jesus was modeling very clearly what we all need to aim for. To experience such Love is to at minimum understand that we are loved and deeply treasured children of God. However it is also an invitation to approximate as much of that same love for all life, as a whole, and for every single component of individual life – you, me, the blade of grass, every atom and molecule, and that person we are sure has gone far astray and injured us. Very often loving ourselves, with all our seeming personality flaws and errors, is quite a process and one of our major blockages to this higher love.

Likewise the Peace was another invitation to reach for that state of being in every moment possible. I needed to accelerate my efforts toward that end. Meditate regularly, use a calm and loving affirmation in your mind, and follow your breath allowing greater serenity to pervade you with each breath. Choose the method and focus that is right for you. This benefits us greatly although all those around us and the entire world will indeed receive healing effects from our efforts as well. Jesus was pointing the way for me in all respects; He was pointing the way for us all.

However, the most powerful aspect of His teaching for me was the Joy. We are asked to become a being of joy in all moments. I'm not yet capable of maintaining a constant joy even though I know who we all are and that the journey home is secure. That is an intellectual knowing. What is needed is the experience of that Joy in our union with our own Soul. Or obviously at a moment of contact with a Higher Being who is already grounded in that state, at a moment of grace and blessing. That is available to us.

Having had that experience, I now often find joy and gratitude in any moment when I am resting in love and light. It is deeply rewarding to hold that space of consciousness - for myself, for others, for the world - to just quietly resonate that quality of being. I'm not able to do that all of the time; not yet.

I'm reminded of one of the Bailey teachings. So very many in the world never know a joyful moment. They are downtrodden and sorrowful. However the energy that is a product of that saddened state needs to be offset with our joy. It is a divine responsibility to emerge from our own darkness and clinging and experience the truth of our being. We are needed to bring greater light to the world. Our light is greater than the darkness. And extending this light is compassion for all of the highest order.

Each day right upon awakening and in early meditation, I vividly recall that vision of Jesus and commit myself to another day of working toward being like Him. I have so far to go to attain His depth of Love, Peace, and Joy; yet we are all on our way, knowingly or unknowingly. When we put our will and our action behind our desire for such purity, the process speeds ahead. As Jesus says in the Course take one step toward Me and I will take nineteen steps toward you. It is a metaphor but one with great truth, meaning and upliftment.

As for the pen, let's not forget the pen, of course I still have and cherish it. And, as it turned out, it was the only item on my list that I had forgotten to pick up. I was looking for a special kind of pen which this was. When in a meditative state, I take it and touch it to my heart or my forehead and His love, support, and guidance flow in. Not that a pen, or any other kind of implement, is required for a blessing to be bestowed on us. Still the pen is exceedingly special to me.

We are invited to share our light in whatever way is most powerful for us. Let us put our daily efforts into living in a state of love, peace and joy in every moment possible. It is a blissful existence and is so very needed in the world.

Chapter 11
Reincarnation: A Useful View of What Ails Us

*M*any of you reading a book of this nature may believe in multiple physical lives. I treasure the Course's perspective on reincarnation discussed in the Teachers Manual of the book. My interpretation of what it says is that it doesn't really matter what our beliefs are about this topic for us to move ahead spiritually. Our primary need is to be working on releasing our fears, false beliefs, and lack of love. So if reincarnation is not your thing, fine. There still may be, however, a few concepts and experiences in this chapter which may be interesting, useful and worth pondering.

Our minds are challenged in that we so often dwell in negative judgments, guilt, fear, blame, despair, and anxiety. If any of you spend an entire hour in your day feeling nothing but love and acceptance for one and all, including yourself, then put down this book and get started on your own, and I want a copy.

To one extent or another all of us are filled with ego beliefs and desires; correcting our misunderstandings should be our main objective. The content of the ego is projected outward, thus creating our very strained worldly condition. That's what I believe the Course's perspective is. And I surely agree – focus on our unhealed inner state and make changes. Of course cosmic concepts, including those on reincarnation, can be very helpful in accomplishing that.

There are reasons why most of us are born with a thick veil shielding us from our other lives. There are wounds, self-blame and pain in us from other experiences and times. However, we already have our share of challenges in this life. So I am not one who advises folks to delve into alternate lives without serious consideration and higher guidance and assistance. My reason for including this discussion is that just knowing this truth often allows us to accept that there is rhyme and reason to all that takes place. That can make our lives much more comfortable. It greatly expands our vision.

As a transpersonal psychologist, I receive frequent requests to do regression therapy and I am sometimes guided to suggest otherwise. If an individual hasn't done sufficient psychological and spiritual work on themselves and their Forgiveness skills aren't up to par, they will very likely come to memories that may be so upsetting that they spend months working through their despair, guilt, and anger. All that being said, there is a great deal of merit in coming to understand that we do have multiple life experiences in this earthly dimension as I mentioned. They are all offered to us by the Universe as experiences for awakening from our ego-ridden mind.

In addition, it is true that in our Soul state, we have agreed to these various adventures. Sometimes we make excellent use of these experiences and sometimes we drag our proverbial feet. It's a tough journey; lots of hills and valleys. All of this has been presented previously in this book and is worthy of continued contemplation.

As multiple life opportunities slowly become a reality for us, we are likely to be more understanding and patient with the trials and events of this life. We may be more forbearing and serene related to the people in our life. Things may start to make more sense. We consider more possibilities. We have unfinished business to complete from other times, although it is unconscious for most of us. We have preparations to make for our future challenges and service.

A physical life is a treasure of great value. Our human lives are very important as there are many processes of awakening that require a human form. As we gradually transform our belief systems, our life's tribulations become easier to bear since we know they have meaning and connections with our past and future and that our Soul knew these experiences to be most useful.

I do realize there is much information today relating to time not being linear – no actual past or future. Actually we're told that there is no time and space at all once we do awaken. The Course states that everything is actually happening at once and our joined minds just lay it all out in a more workable format. The experience of time is very different in various dimensions; I know that to be true. These are all very challenging concepts. However, our experience right here and now is one of linear time, so I will speak in this chapter from that perspective.

I'd like to share a few thoughts about my personal experiences. I had not given reincarnation much thought in my twenties. However, over forty years ago, largely for stress management purposes and because the Beatles had done it, I began meditating. Since it was expensive to learn to meditate at that time and I was a starving graduate student, when I finally saved enough money to learn the practice, I became very compulsive about doing what I'd been taught.

So twice a day for twenty minutes I did my Transcendental Meditation mantra and found great merit to the method. I had been practicing diligently for some good amount of time when I occasionally had memories surface that seemed to be me in other lives. Sometimes I would have dreams that contained remnants of similar memories. I make no attempt to convince anyone else of their validity. But I will say that each memory came as a teaching – something that I needed to understand, accept, and often Forgive to accelerate my journey. They were extremely helpful but sometimes very difficult to cope with.

Through the decades I have purposefully or accidentally bumped into alternate lives in a variety of ways. As I said above, sometimes it would be in meditation or occasional dreams that had a particularly compelling and elucidating nature about them. I have worked with one psychiatrist and one physician who had been investigating past lives and much of that forthcoming material was enlightening to me.

My MAP Team has brought several lives to my attention, which contained very strong negative experiences, and were emotionally, spiritually, and physically adversely affecting me in this life. That group of advanced beings has been invaluable to me in clearing away more and more of the debris of my lower mind connected to those other lives and I have been further healed and unburdened. More of that work is to come I imagine.

I felt humbled in finding that some of my opinions in this life that I thought were based purely on wise reasoning actually had wounded, unfinished experiences at their base from other times. An example would be that I have long felt that it is such a waste to spend so much money on lavish weddings when children all over the world are hungry and starving. I feel that way about many things we spend excessive amounts of funds on. Most of us are rather self-centered and often put our ego desires first. Money is needed for so many worthy and crucial purposes to help our world. And I will admit I still feel that way.

I have been married twice with very small weddings each time and they have been satisfying to me and right for my belief system. However, through deeper subconscious work, I identified a painful memory connected to a rather lavishly planned wedding in my own past. I had been left at the altar as they say. The remnants of that experience had not been entirely forgiven and were influencing my current belief system. Learning that was definitely humbling and informative. Any experience that reduces my attachment to my own opinions and judgments is great stuff. This is just one example of many treasures found and healed in my subconscious through the years. This awareness has changed many of my viewpoints although obviously not all, and has definitely quieted my busy opinionated mind.

Occasionally there has been a purely spontaneous memory occurring seemingly out of nowhere. I recall a day when I was in the kitchen making soup and listening to classical music. Ave Maria began to play and, as bizarre as this will sound, I gradually fell to the floor in fear, sobbing my heart out. As I began to calm down, I witnessed in my mind a distant memory when I was a young nun in Europe, having entered the convent unwillingly and subsequently ran away. I had been found and brought back to the convent and punished severely.

That lifetime was not one of my favorites. I was now being asked by my Soul however to accept and Forgive all that it contained knowing the importance of the experience.

It is valuable here to mention that I have never had an experience come upon me where I could not choose how to deal with it. It might sound frightening to read about falling to the floor and sobbing. Reactions like that are not what most of us want emerging unexpectedly. However, my experience is that when I feel something like that coming on, which rarely occurs, I can choose not to display any physical reaction to it. Perhaps I will appear to be rather temporarily distracted to others present but that's about it. So don't let my experience be a cautionary one for you.

But it is also true that if my circumstances permit the privacy, it is wise to really feel the full impact of what is being presented and that allows for quicker, deeper healing. We need to safely release those deeply pent up emotions. They usually scare us going in but I have always felt immensely released and renewed after the occasion even though perhaps temporarily a little tired. This is likewise true of the clients I have worked with to these ends. So again please don't let these moments in my life be frightening in any way. I've given permission to my MAP Team to go for it with me when the right timing presents itself. Their assistance with the process is, as always, invaluable.

Actually I had a rather strange experience just some months ago that remains spectacularly clear in my mind. I was walking through a grocery store parking lot. There was a bench outside the entry door and sitting on it was, to my mind, one of the most beautiful humans I had ever seen. He was very large and well proportioned, likely in his thirties, and the best way I can describe him further is that he was straight out of an Incan painting. His coloring and facial structure were precisely as I remembered them.

Now when I say I remembered them I mean that at the moment I saw him, he seemed very familiar to me. I had an intensely powerful impulse to run to him, kneel at his feet, and ask him how I could serve him. Fortunately I am somewhat accustomed to having a few strange experiences here and there, so I do have self-control and don't act out every impulse.

At the same time I felt this, I saw clearly in my mind a lifetime in which I was a member of a culture that had served his culture. I was essentially a slave to these people and I revered them as gods. I stood completely still and allowed all of this memory and feeling to pass through me. But in truth I wanted nothing more than to kneel before him in joyful abject servitude. He was just so very beautiful to me! I see him in my mind right now. It was only my inner guidance that told me to leave well enough alone – that no action was wise action in that moment. It was difficult to finally walk into the store.

At this point I have partial recall of about nineteen lives, not all of which were on this planet but mostly so. The material I recall all seemed to point me toward an event or circumstance that I had not completely Forgiven and released and still had some negative impact on me. So there was always work to be done. Sometimes it was others I needed to Forgive and sometimes it was me. We have many subconscious wounds and pains. We, of course, also have many wonderful and enjoyable lives and experiences in our subconscious memory bank as well. I place here more emphasis on the educational aspects of our recalled material but there have been a lot of very comfortable and satisfying times in our past. We have learned from those too.

I'm going to mention just two more of the lives I recall because working with that content has been so profound for me in the last few years. Both of these lives were brought to me by my MAP Team with my permission. Things are seldom forced upon us and always the Soul agrees through higher wisdom. These lives occurred back to back hundreds of years ago.

In the first life I was a slave who had been placed in charge of other slaves and their work output. My privileges depended on their production. I was ruthless and often cruel. I was afraid of being placed again in even worse conditions than I had been in before if I did not fulfill my owner's expectations. I hurt many people because of my fear. At some level fear always underlies negative thoughts and actions. I continued with that hurtful behavior throughout that life. I died angry and afraid.

In my succeeding life and, I am told, the hardest of all my lives, I was again a slave primarily used for breeding purposes. I was a child-bearing machine. I gave birth to many children and by the age of four or five, they were then sold to others for whatever their purposes might be. I do not recall a time in that life when I was not in emotional and physical anguish. My anger knew no bounds within myself although my behavior had to remain completely controlled to avoid greater pain and deprivation. I developed many health problems and died with no understanding of my plight in any way. I have believed for many years, maintaining great compassion for us all, that there are no victims. There's purpose behind everything. Coming to understand this lifetime as connected to the previous one reinforced that belief tremendously.

Reviewing and re-experiencing parts of those lives were among my most difficult times in recent years. Some of my emotional reactions and health problems in this life were remnants of those other lives. I was surprised how strongly my present physical health was related to my illnesses of my breeder-slave existence. My current health and expansion of consciousness depended on my understanding, accepting, and Forgiving myself and others connected to those times. I still had psychic connections to some of the children I bore then and needed to help them to heal their still-existing pain, although obviously they had gone on to other physical forms long ago in terms of linear time. Helping others can be psychically done; we're all connected within. It truly is a test of our love.

It is clear to me that many of our current health problems, physical and emotional, are related to old, unhealed personal material from this life or another. That's really been proven to me through much of my work on myself and work I have done with others in psychotherapy. We carry pain with us and it affects all dimensions of who we are currently.

It has been immensely gratifying to observe others be relieved of some of their woes through such past recognition. One thing that stands out for me is that so often people recognize individuals in their other lives as people they are currently connected with as well. They see the reversal of roles and become aware of the karmic interplay of what has taken place. It gives all of us a more enlightened perspective on current conditions and relationships. When we see ourselves doing the same thing we are so enraged about now in someone else, it gives us much pause for reconsideration.

I have to say again I am not advocating that people purposefully seek out these experiences unless they have rather clear Higher Guidance to do so and a methodology to assist in the process (hopefully a MAP Team). Only then move forward with love, acceptance, and caution. Many folks feel more comfortable in doing this kind of work with a healer or mental health practitioner who has experience in these matters. Often it is the unhealed material that surfaces most prevalently in our consciousness. That is where our major work lies. It is best not to enter those domains without a Forgiving and wise heart and a good Soul connection.

I also wish to add that I dearly love and believe the "Course" perspective on our miseries and pains no matter what period they derive from. To my understanding it states that truly worthy work is to attain the ultimate Forgiveness as discussed a few chapters back. When we actually awaken to the universal reality that there is nothing left to Forgive, everything unhealed from our "past" is automatically cleared away. I'm not saying it happens when we just believe that concept intellectually, but rather when it has deepened into every fiber of our consciousness so that Forgiveness of everything is actually attained through our wisdom.

Delving into our own so-called "past" is just one option for further healing and awakening. Working with ultimate truths, meditating, and nourishing our growing awareness is the truly crucial work. If for some reason the memories are brought to us, we can choose to reach for that more advanced guidance and work with them as well as we are able. Our recognition that alternate lives do exist, and for good purpose, can bring greater peace and patience into our lives today.

However, all that being said, I will tell you that just in recent times I've had the good fortune of discovering an excellent book by Gordon Davidson called *Joyful Evolution* which stems from an advanced arena of knowledge he has titled "Multi-dimensional Psychology". Gordon shares teachings and many methods and meditations for enhancing our inner connection with our subconscious and our Soul. He gives us practices and paths that lead to healing of our old wounds. This is a fine work that affords us methodology to quicken this healing process which involves the unifying of our superconscious, conscious, and subconscious minds. If this is an area that interests you, please do examine this work; it can be found at www.joyfulevolution.net.

Now in the following chapter, I am going to delve into more challenging possibilities that can easily boggle our minds. They certainly have demanded my best scrutiny, inner discrimination and Soul wisdom.

Chapter 12
Challenging Perspectives
on Alternate Realities

*I*n this chapter we'll travel further down the ole rabbit hole and consider some of the other angles on reincarnation. There are more scientific and experiential suggestions than ever before that multiple dimensions of reality do exist. Whether we talk about parallel universes, or probable realities, or past or future lives, it is all recognition that there is more to the depths of our consciousness than we are even remotely aware of. Indeed, talking about this at all is challenging; we lack common vocabulary, definitions and understandings. No doubt a physicist would do far better than I on this topic. But then I'm not sure how many of us would understand what we read.

A few decades back, I thoroughly enjoyed reading the Seth material which came through Jane Roberts. I believe there are important truths contained in her many books. One of the concepts that really played out well for me in trying to understand my own experiences was that of "probable realities". What I recall of Seth's discussion of that is that our minds can try out several paths of experience at one time for the purpose of enhancing our learning possibilities. Actually when I read back what I just wrote, this last sentence would apply to any of the alternate dimensions we are talking about in these chapters. Clearly, for most of us, these are unconscious activities.

In a few of my altered states, I have briefly resided in a probable reality in which my beloved spouse and I have not gotten along well and finally gave up the effort. In another we again had much conflict between us but stayed together and made each other's lives miserable. We seemed to be learning little that I could discern in either of these glimpses but in truth we likely were and are. The reality I live in each day with him is our best outcome so far it would appear. We have differences but are both serious about our spiritual awakening and actually get along well. We seem to be closer as the years go by. These various avenues of reality for the two of us have all been very vivid to me.

Increasingly as the years go by, I find myself occasionally functioning in a different dimension simultaneously to this earth experience as I've mentioned. Sometimes I am learning by witnessing how other dimensions operate, sometimes I am sent to assist in some way as part of my training, and sometimes I see myself living out a separate life in that alternate space of consciousness. At times I really want to remain there when I find it to be an environment of greater peace and harmony among all. At first when the veil would thin and I would pick up on any of these other experiences, I would freak and the image would immediately disappear. I am just now getting a little better at holding both realities at once.

I have come to understand that I am merely witnessing these actions; that my Higher Self is in charge and working through whatever vehicle deemed appropriate at that moment, perhaps through many. I continue to work on my ability to hold more than one dimension of consciousness at a time. It will be a required skill someday as we travel further on our road of higher awareness. I've really got a long way to go on this one.

Let's move on to another challenging concept. A number of very advanced materials, *A Course in Miracles* and the Bailey works included, suggest that all of this experience I'm speaking of in this chapter on reincarnation is an illusion – a concept that many of us find bizarre and confusing. And we've heard suggestions of that nature from the scientific community as well. But what is meant by that? Not being very scientifically minded, my best understanding of that is connected to our concept of God and the vast hierarchy of beings that have sprung from God.

I firmly believe that anyone currently in human form is ill equipped to grasp the mysteries of the universe. There are purposes and processes far beyond our ability to understand. The simplest way I am able to express my discernment on this issue of illusion is that the Prime Source of the universe has created innumerable beings with creative powers as well. These creative powers are meant to be used throughout our journey of awakening as an important aspect of our gaining Godly perfection in the end. We are meant to use our free will to make better and better choices in making our world(s).

The teachings I revere use the word illusion to designate anything made by the beings God created. Only what our Prime Source created is eternal. All else is temporary though it be billions of years old in many cases, again linearly speaking. Illusion is temporarily made by the mental creative facility of beings young and old in Soul. So in the Course for example the word illusion connotes temporality – not being eternal.

So if I'm making any sense here at all, keep in mind that whatever dimensions, or universes, or realities we might discuss or experience are temporary and of the illusory world. Eckhart Tolle poetically uses the phrase "collective dream". It is a long learning, remembering drama created by our joined minds. The remembering aspect is very important to emphasize because deep within us, we know the mysteries of the universe. The place where our Higher Mind has always been connected to God is not unclear about these things. Our learning experiences bring us ever nearer to our remembrance of those Cosmic Truths through union with our Soul and beyond.

Thinking of this world as an illusion in no way makes it trivial. As I have stated before, there are crucial aspects of our journey home that must take place under these circumstances. It is not a demeaning understanding of the value of worldly experience. Should we choose to take this perspective into our heart and mind, as I do, it can be another consideration that lightens our load as we travel. We might take it all less intensely while still giving it our best.

To take these ponderous considerations a little further, I will add that there is growing evidence that all time co-exists simultaneously. Even Einstein suggested this. That would indicate that our superconscious joined minds create time – past, present, and future. And that we will reach a level of reality where all of those separating veils will disappear.

If this is so, and I am certainly impressed by the sources these teachings come from including *A Course in Miracles*, it may suggest the idea that our current mind states can affect what we commonly think of as the past. In a way it may be possible in some form for us to remake our "past" and bring greater healing to our whole being and to others. I am reminded here of the work I was asked to do with my "children" of my breeder slave life. Perhaps truly Forgiving a past event actually changes it in some important way. Some of the science fiction films available today that seem to convey bizarre scenarios may have some little bit of truth to them, or more. This is all very mysterious stuff and poorly understood as yet.

However, teachings are clear that in our Divine Eternal Self, our Higher Mind and beyond, we have never left our home, our union with God. That is what this entire journey, certainly the point of this little book, is about - supporting us in moving forward and once again experientially realizing our union with God. We would then be a tried and true Soul with the wisdom of the ages and endless experience contained within our consciousness. At that point, all of these strange avenues of reality will become clear to us in their truth or error. I'm sure we don't understand it all correctly in our current state of awareness. Well, that's my best shot on all of this.

However I wish to add as an after-thought that in numerous wise passages, it is said that words shared by humans can convey very little of the ultimate universal truths. Words are symbols of thoughts which in turn are also symbols of higher realities. There are layers upon layers. Words are like pointers toward a yet vague understanding of how things work and what the journey is about. This is well worth remembering as we venture down unknown trails. There's no doubt that Initiates of the Higher Way gradually grasp the actuality that we only very minimally understand, but our day will come. So let us relax knowing the grand and benign nature of our path home and that we are guided all the way. All is well.

Chapter 13
The World Teacher: A Guide to Our Future

R eminiscent of Chapter 9 focusing on the magnificent divine help available to us all, please allow me to share with you a prophecy that I find deeply inspiring and exciting. Many of us believe that we now stand on the verge of a great transformation in the consciousness of humankind. I surely believe that and think we have been moving along that path for some time. We have greater assistance in achieving these goals than most of us have begun to consider.

About thirty-five years ago I was exposed to very ancient, challenging and awe-inspiring materials. The major portions of these were sections of the Vedas, the four or five thousand year old scriptures held sacred by many in the East and now sacred to many world-wide. That was the first time I encountered the concept of a great World Teacher coming physically into our midst at the beginning of each new astronomical age. That Teacher walks among us at those times to dispense a more advanced spiritual understanding of who we are and what is needed to enlighten the world. It was said that humanity is thought to be capable of expanding its spiritual understanding further at those crucial times. We now stand at the beginning of the Aquarian Age. It was suggested that this would be one of those times when this miraculous event would unfold.

A few years went by and I became more deeply involved in the Alice Bailey studies. These are briefly described in Chapter 8. Among the first six or seven Bailey books I examined was her book entitled *The Reappearance of the Christ*. I must repeat that the term "Christ" is used here with a more expanded meaning than is usually ascribed to it. Most of us have heard and read the phrase "Jesus the Christ". That expression suggests that "the Christ" is a title, perhaps a position held. That is just what was discussed in the Bailey book. It explained what I had read earlier in the Vedic scriptures that at the beginning of every new age a World Teacher, advanced beyond our capacity to understand, comes again to walk among us and teach us how to heal ourselves and the world, and how to move forward.

I believe this is an idea that many have heard and have had varying reactions. Some reject the concept because they feel that our work is to develop the "Christ Consciousness" within ourselves and not to look outward for guidance and awakening. Indeed this emerging consciousness within is crucially important and could be greatly aided by the emergence of a great teacher. Others, of course, generally reject this idea as totally preposterous on principle alone. And still others reject it because it does not fit their currently formed ideas of how the Christ will return to the world. We all are invited to form our own conclusions.

The Bailey book asserted that the World Teacher, who indeed does hold the position of the Christ (the title for the head of our Spiritual Hierarchy, our Masters of Wisdom), does come to us to show the way to develop our union with our Higher Self, our Soul. It is said that He comes not to repair the staggering woes of our world but to help us do what we are capable of doing – change our values, develop love for all in our hearts and actions, and move forward to change all the dysfunctional systems of our world. Yes, we must develop our "Christ Consciousness" within and guidance and support in this endeavor is greatly needed.

I felt tremendously heartened by this. I didn't know if it was true. However, I had found great veracity and direction that really made a wonderful difference for me in the teachings of the other Bailey books. So I was certainly open to this being an upcoming reality. I felt this way in spite of the predictions that great trials and tribulations would beset us all in the years preceding our movement into a more spiritually expanded world. Many prophecies included geophysical abnormalities and catastrophes as well as the breakdown of many of our institutions and governments which no longer served the welfare of all people. We seem to be in the midst of these changes at this time.

Then in 1980 I read a book entitled *The Reappearance of the Christ and the Masters of Wisdom* by an English esotericist, Benjamin Crème. This excellent book took the concept several steps further stating that this unparalleled time in our human history would not only bring forth the World Teacher but additionally many of the Masters of Wisdom would come forward in physical form to aid the effort as well.

Many of us do see clearly that the world is headed in a downward spiral due to the increasingly negative value system that predominates. Separatism and working only for the short-sighted good of ourselves or our particular group, be that family, community, or nation, seems to rule our behavior. And that's assuming that most are working for the good at all, which most of us would challenge. We certainly need this divine guidance to understand that we must heal and come together world-wide in brotherhood for survival, and because our Oneness is an actual higher truth.

Of course, thankfully, this separatism does not characterize the views and actions of us all. This past year of 2011 has frequently illustrated the increasing world-wide desire for a better life based on more advanced principles of living for many more people. Thousands have been willing to die or risk their lives to ensure this outcome. It is a time of much inspiration and much demonstration of wisdom and courage.

However, recognizing our global connection, indeed our spiritual oneness, and working for the good of all has been minimally emphasized and adhered to. When the World Teacher espoused a value system that embraced this union, I was greatly uplifted. His axiom "without sharing, there is no justice and without justice, there is no peace" represented a truth important and profound. It contained an obvious answer to the world's problems, obvious but not easily accomplished. When I say espoused, I am referring to a number of writings said to be given us by the World Teacher and relayed by Benjamin Crème. These teachings have been vastly inspiring to me.

However, it is additionally stated in these materials that in contrast to appearances, if humanity but knew, many have moved forward in their conscious awareness with great strides in these last few centuries. That with all our woes and errors of today, we are still much more advanced in many ways than in times gone by. Therefore, we are more prepared than we might think to make this great leap forward in consciousness which is needed to save and heal the world. I pray this is all so and believe that it is.

Benjamin Crème believes the World Teacher is already with us, very slowly coming forward, anonymously at this time, and reaching out to all with loving energy and wise counsel. The World Teacher does not interfere with our free will and, of course, does and will allow each individual to work with this information, energy and transformation in their own way.

I have followed this story for many years, have read the materials speaking of it, and have attended many national conferences discussing this emergence of the World Teacher. I have always been very favorably affected by every aspect of this. My meditation at these conferences has been of the finest I have had the privilege to experience and very healing to all aspects of my being. Many of the predictions to come from this movement have come to pass although not all.

There are many in the world who believe this all to be true. For that matter, many world religions are expecting a great teacher to arrive on our chaotic and fear-filled scene. Let us seek whether there is openness in our hearts for this possibility and, if so, be watchful for the higher guidance and direction that may be on our doorstep. My heart and Soul yearn for this event and fulfillment. It is time to restore God's plan on our earth. Actually it is a dire necessity. For those of you who have interest in further inquiry on this topic, much interesting information can be found at www.share-international.org/. On this page I have offered for your inspection and perhaps adoption the prayer that many of us say daily related to this momentous event and the healing of our world.

THE GREAT INVOCATION

From the point of Light within the Mind of God
Let Light stream forth into the minds of men.
Let Light descend on Earth.

From the point of Love within the Heart of God
Let Love stream forth into the hearts of men.
May Christ return to Earth.

From the Centre where the Will of God is known
Let purpose guide the little wills of men –
The Purpose which the Masters know and serve.

From the Centre which we call the race of men
Let the Plan of Love and Light work out.
And may it seal the door where evil dwells.

Let Light and Love and Power
Restore the Plan on Earth.

Chapter 14
Gratitude Gathering Force

*A*s we know this book is a series of essays or thoughts for pondering. I placed this essay here because I am so grateful for all the teachings and realizations shared in the previous chapters. And because for most of our many lives there has been much hardship and challenge. Certainly that is true for many people today. Without wisdom and understanding, earth experience is felt to be a very difficult path. If, in wisdom, we can cultivate gratitude, it eases our burdens. There is so much to be grateful for in our lives that is not apparent to most of us.

Only our awakening to the nature of our path brings about relief from the suffering and desires of this world. Our cultivation of gratitude travels through stages of awareness throughout our existence. For most of our time spent in the earthly state of consciousness, there is little or no gratitude in our mental frame of reference. That is the first stage. We feel strongly besieged by the trials and tribulations of our physical and emotional lives. It is quite understandable.

As we move closer to our initial spiritual awakening, we start to lighten up a bit and become conscious of the many gifts that are in our lives. Perhaps we notice more of what has always been there or have a slightly different take on what surrounds us now. This is the second stage of gratitude. Our gratitude is focused on being aware of having the things that make our egos more comfortable in this world.

This usually includes gratitude for wealth and possessions, worldly success, as well as our health and the health and welfare of those we love, and so on. It is focused on all the "good" stuff that makes our lives easier and more pleasant. This is clearly an advance in thinking over the many lives we spent in stage one feeling strongly victimized, anxious, and angry. And there are surely many times when no gratitude continues to dominate.

In the third stage, we make strides in waking up to the higher realities, who we really are and why we are here. This is the stage where we truly start to understand that wonderful Course statement that we don't know what lies in our own best interests. We start to contemplate that we are here to spiritually move forward and advance in consciousness. We have no idea what experiences and circumstances will produce the finest results and what happenings offer us the best opportunities. We start to get it.

In this third stage we are grateful for much more than in the second. When something troublesome comes our way, we may grumble and gripe but we begin to be appreciative of the chance to gain more insight within ourselves, perhaps heal another wound.

Another Course statement we have often contemplated in our studies and gatherings, sometimes laughing and sometimes not, goes something like bow down to whomever or whatever has upset, angered, or irritated you the most today for that is your finest teacher of this moment. All our negative emotions point to something unhealed and unaccepted within ourselves. Few people believe this. It is not a statement that we no longer recognize wrongful things in the world. However when we are healed within, we observe and deal with those events from a space of inner peace and wisdom. Our critical judgment is diminished.

Thus now we feel gratitude for even the tough times. We begin to awaken to their potential. We seriously want to expand our consciousness. We're not delighted with troubles; we seldom say "bring it on". We are, however, cooperating with our Soul and the meaning of life; our resistance and struggle is much reduced. That means we are more comfortable by far.

Just recently a friend was sharing with me that he had undergone a serious illness. David had felt angry, confused, and frightened. And sick. It took months for him to begin to recover. He had to learn to slow down and let go of many of his non-essentials in possessions and activities. He was experiencing what it was like to think and act in terms of taking good care of himself. By the time we were having this conversation, David loved the changes he had made! His present existence felt like a whole new life to him. He made time for his own self-care in body, mind, and spirit. He was expressing gratitude for being forced into a lifestyle he now greatly valued but would not have chosen without the illness. A super stage three experience!

We're closing in on stage four at this point. Here our wisdom is deepening further. Our attachment to worldly gratification is very much diminishing. We have desires but they have mostly risen to our wanting true spiritual attainment more than anything. We have much less interest in our possessions and successes, our lows and highs; we see with greater equilibrium.

Our gratitude has now shifted to a deep reverence and appreciation that there is more than this life, this level of consciousness. We are so thankful that there is a path home to enlightenment, that there are Beings ahead of us giving our development Their all. We are appreciative that we are never alone and that we are deeply realizing the true purpose of existence. It is exhilarating and so freeing! We can truly live more fully the statement I shared with you earlier made by the great teacher of the twentieth century, J. Krishnamurti, that he did not mind how things are. It was his casual way of saying that there is a spiritual perfection we do not yet fully recognize or understand. In this stage we not only know there is rhyme and reason for what takes place but we are also living a state founded in a higher dimension.

There is little that can be said through our human communication about stage five. In this stage we now actually attain a full awakening. We experience a union with all things. We are at peace and feel whole in Spirit. There is much joy and love. There is no longer any sense of separation or attachment. Gratitude is usually experienced for something or someone distinct from ourselves. Now we are that one Divine Someone. We are in oneness with God. The bliss has replaced separativeness. Union has replaced gratitude.

We can easily pass through most of these stages in one life (maybe in one moody, challenging day) although stage five takes a while to attain and stabilize. Or we may stay in one stage our entire life. However, eventually full attainment of love and wisdom is gained or rather remembered from within where we have known all this always. We can nurture our forward movement in gratitude through our perspective on many experiences that come our way or spiritual practices we choose to adopt. It is all a natural flow forward.

In one workshop I presented, we all had a great time comparing these five stages with the five stages of achieving serenity in Chapter 3. There are numerous parallels and folks valued comparing the content of each stage to how they felt and acted during a typical day or a particularly upsetting occurrence. It was very enlightening and motivating!

So we might ask ourselves what stage do we spend most of our time in. Where would we like to be? What are we willing to do to get there? These questions are worth asking ourselves in our most quiet and reflective moments. We will have a great deal of heavenly help in answering them and making our choices to move forward from there.

Chapter 15
Leeda: Spiritual Direction in a Name

I'm indulging myself with this little chapter. It's fun to tell. And it is placed well after the gratitude chapter since I am so appreciative of what follows. A lot of pleasure, inspiration, and guidance have come to me during this life through various names given me.

I was born during WW II to unmarried persons who went their separate ways. That was considered a much more serious event in the 40s than it is today. My biological mother spent her months of pregnancy in a facility connected to a foundling home. That was the phrase used then for a home where single mothers could place their babies for adoption. She left promptly after my birth, which I feel was a very wise decision on her part. The Catholic nuns there named me Bridget, a good Irish name for a little Irish lass. I've always been very fond of that name.

When sometime after that I was adopted, my adoptive parents named me Dorothy. It means, my Mother told me, "gift from God". And that's how my adoptive Mother felt about me after wanting a child for so many years and her wishes being fulfilled. I was very fortunate she felt that way and benefited greatly from her love and care.

I was raised in the Catholic faith so when I was ten or eleven, I was allowed to choose a confirmation name and I chose Helena which was rather strange even for that time period. But a few decades later I really valued the choice when I began to read the works of Helena Blavatsky and Helena Roerich. There was challenging but magnificent material in those books. I felt pleasure from having that as my confirmation name and I've always wondered a bit about where that choice came from in my consciousness.

While completing my Ph.D., I worked temporarily in a federal prison. The Black Muslims there gave me the name of Sakinah, which I enjoyed and found beautiful to my mind and my ear. I felt honored and still do especially since I am Caucasian. I felt very fortunate that they accepted me in some way, that we did have some kind of connection. I will always treasure that.

In the late 70s I was privileged to connect with a great spiritual leader, Swami Muktananda. We called Him Baba and I can't begin to recount the spiritual teachings and experiences I received from Him in the following years until He left His body in the early 80s. What a great Initiate – One who could give His disciples the experience of their Higher Self, the Soul, with a touch or a look, perhaps a thought as well. Those receiving that blessing were never the same after that gift. That was a deep and advanced path to awakening for me.

He would give his devotees a spiritual name. Mine was Neelima, which means "blue person" referring to Krishna. I loved it and it continues to be sacred to me. That was a very significant chapter in my spiritual growth. Baba is the Guru of the great spiritual personage of today, Swami Chidvilasananda often called Gurumayi, who is the head of the Siddha Yoga Foundation. Both these great Initiates have given us wonderful blessings and materials to study and an excellent meditation practice. The Foundation is very worthy of investigation, my friends.

Now we come to the central reason I wanted to share this little piece. This is one example of the many teachings, practices, and support that my MAP Team has offered me through the years. (Our chapter on MAP coming up a little later. I know I keep saying that but it really is.) The "problem list" we give our MAP Team is taken very seriously and moving forward spiritually has always been on my list. So at one point in my MAPing sessions I began to hear the word "Leeda". Gradually I came to know this was kind of a pet name they called me. In reality it was rather more of a "working title" for me if I can use the term so loosely.

Each letter of the name stood for a quality I was and am working on within myself. It was offered to me as a learning device or mantra to repeat many times a day for bringing myself back to my task of holding proper consciousness. I offer seminars, coordinate several spiritual study groups and a meditation group, and do energy work with people in addition to transpersonal counseling. At first, I thought Leeda was to be focused on more at those times, during my work hours. However, my MAP buddies have encouraged me to strive for a constant "Leeda" state of awareness. I'll be working on that for the remainder of this life to be sure. It is a beautiful journey – a journey we all are on.

Here's what the name stands for. "L" represents loving. We are asked to see through the human personality to the Divine Soul that we all truly are. We are asked not to be fooled into limited thinking that anyone is just a body with a personality. That's the least of who we are and with that perspective held in mind, it is much easier to love ourselves and others. This is an ongoing goal. It is not the type of love that most of us experience in this world but rather a Divine Love that is a benign and active caring for all life. We've spoken of this desirable mind set before.

The first "E" stands for effortless. I tend to push myself too much. I tend to think I'm not doing enough. I've joked with friends for years that my tombstone, were I to have one which I won't, would read "She Tried Too Hard". I'm slowly chipping away at that and it feels great to let go more and more. Clearly there has been much fear underlying some of those efforts and healing has been needed and much has been accomplished. Spiritually speaking, we are asked to get our egos out of the way and let our Soul do Its work in the world. That's an effortless and joyful state to be in. I grasp the divine teaching that he who thinks he is the doer is a fool. He here refers to the lower self.

A spiritual motto I encountered decades ago still inspires me to live its very simple message: "striving ceases". It points to a certain juncture in our spiritual journey wherein we have surrendered to the energy and action of our Divine Self, surrendered to the Will of God. "Striving ceases" does not mean that we cease our spiritual practices or our ongoing Self-awareness or our Soul-inspired activities in the world. I can't remember which spiritual teacher said that the Kingdom of God is effortless. Resting in Spirit is the goal and all else flows through.

The second "E" stands for equanimity. I need to remain peaceful in all I do, to not allow the emotions and thoughts of the lower self take control. I imagine we all know that is the work of many lives. In fact, I feel all of Leeda's teaching is certainly that. Our desires keep our thoughts and feelings very active and peace rather distant and rare. My lack of peace interferes with being a more pure servant of the Light.

"D" stands for detachment. What aids me most in this is that I really do believe we do not know what any proper outcome is at this human level. When I remember that my work is just to listen for my Soul's guidance, detachment becomes much more doable if not automatic.

Detachment does not mean not caring. We can love deeply while still retaining the knowledge that we don't know what is right for another's experience. We seldom know what is most productive for our own. As we progress in our consciousness, there is more "witnessing" and "observing" of the flow of things rather than being attached to each turn and twist. Deep compassion for our human condition surely remains.

And lastly the "A" stands for alignment. I have heard within that the other four are less purely carried out if we are not aligned with our Soul. Meditation has been my springboard to that alignment for many years. There surely are others. Continued effort for that Soul union is gradually leading us to a more constant alignment with our Higher Mind where a wise knowing of what to think, feel, and do is clear.

So the word "Leeda" is a wonderful instant reminder and realignment with all I strive for. Many people experience that through their meditation mantra or favorite prayer. We all need a meaningful word or phrase that takes us back to the truth. Consider choosing one that is instantly uplifting to you and keep it moving through your mind. It is an immediate consciousness-raising activity.

Chapter 16
On Being Empty-Headed

This was a fun seminar to do. It just lends itself to a few chuckles. However, it is a serious issue. So much of our advancement on our spiritual journey rests on emptying out our lower mind, the domain of the ego. No small task whatsoever, but is entirely possible with sustained effort and actually it is required to seriously get on with awakening. Empty headed refers to creating stillness within our mind—a prize of great worth.

A dear friend of mine coordinates a Zen Meditation group and sends out a weekly reminder email. He inserts very funny and relevant cartoons. They are a joy. The last one showed a meditation student standing in front of his teacher who is saying to him "I've never known anyone as thoughtless as you are. You are doing very well, my son".

Most of us are relatively aware that we usually think, feel, and act from our lower mind. Our ego territory is usually a rather busy place filled with desires, judgments, the past and future, fears, planning, and often many resentments as well. And, too, there are delicious fantasies of wonderful things to be done or attained which keep us working toward the wrong goals. The decisions that we normally make from our habitual lower mind are far too tainted by what the world has taught us to believe and desire. We can and must upgrade that belief system.

The first step that many of us likely accomplished was becoming sufficiently still to hear our minds just yapping away. We are usually run by our habitual thoughts. Few of us have yet taken charge of our mental content. For most of us, we quickly hear that an unusually high percentage of our thoughts are useless, repetitive, and even depressing or anxiety producing. If we dig deep enough, we usually find that many of our thoughts do not even represent anything akin to truth. We just get lost in our ego perception of things, usually developed by our past experiences, and go round and round.

There are many fine sources of help with this condition. I am reminded of the works of Eckhart Tolle and Jon Kabat-Zinn. Their methods are invaluable for bringing awareness to the activities of our mind. Dropping back to a gentle awareness of our breath and allowing our focus to remain there as long as possible goes a long way in breaking our addiction to constant and habitual thought. It creates that reflective space that we need.

This awareness allows us the opportunity to be in touch with our present moment. This deeper self-awareness can be a doorway to the experience of our true inner self - a place of much greater peace and wholeness. I cannot speak too highly of studying Tolle's and Kabat-Zinn's books and practicing what they suggest. Doorways to freedom and higher awareness abound in those pages.

There is much to be said for the repetition of sound spiritual concepts so that we are able to grasp them intellectually. You know I'm a fan of that. Then a great deal more study and practice is needed to have them become a reality in our entirety. Many of the concepts we have discussed in earlier chapters apply to being more empty headed - creating greater stillness and serenity in ourselves.

I think it may have been in the late seventies when I first attended a silent mindfulness meditation retreat. It wasn't easy and I will admit a dear friend of mine and I met occasionally in the laundry room after lights out to share our misery. I would plot as to how to have someone call and say I must return home immediately. I didn't carry out those plans of course but it felt good to talk about the possibility and commiserate together. Being stuck with nothing but our own often miserable thoughts many hours a day is no picnic, but highly instructional.

Many hours a day we sat or walked silently doing our best to remain aware of the many passing thoughts in our minds. Actually it was a win if they were passing rather than lingering. We were familiarizing ourselves with their nature and practicing detachment from their content. We began to see their false basis. I remember many years ago a meditation teacher commenting that we are not responsible for every thought that crosses our mind, only the ones we embrace. We were diligently practicing "no embrace". I still sometimes use that phrase as a reminder to break free from those unworthy thoughts that crop up so very often.

I'd been meditating for some years by the time of that retreat so I was a bit staggered at the innumerable thoughts of judgment, fear, guilt, resentment, past, future, and planning I observed in myself. I could see that most of the repetitive planning was just an anxiety reducer and closely related to fear. Judging myself negatively came in a close second in terms of my inner torment.

This deeper, more sustained glimpse into the workings of my mind was very elucidating. Not only did it make clearer to me that I had much more work to do with my emotional healing and mental awareness in daily life, but additionally it showed me that I was merely giving lip-service to many of the spiritual concepts I had been working with. My mind was filled with judgments.

As we have discussed, the Course offers us alternative viewpoints about what makes the world go round. I intellectually had come to believe that there was meaning and opportunity in the events of our lives. I believed I had agreed through my Soul's guidance to undertake this journey just as it was designed and for very good reasons. I also believed I could make it all more difficult for myself with wrong thinking and action. And I often did.

It was so helpful to me to remember that I didn't know what really was in anyone's best interests. Are you tired of hearing that idea yet? What I deemed "bad" sometimes produced the greatest growth in myself or another. And what I deemed "great" often was simply an ego gratification that side tracked me from awakening. Gradually my undeserved confidence in my appraisal of things began to melt away into less judgment and greater serenity.

I had also come to understand and accept that what troubled me about others and the world was often connected to unforgiven and often unconscious issues within myself. A great test of this is for us to observe how emotionally upset we become when confronted with something objectionable. The more upset we are, very often the more it is a reflection of some issue remaining unaddressed within us. I know that I am repeating these concepts again and again throughout this work and I do this quite purposefully. We need to think about them from different angles for most of them to make an impact.

Here's another productive concept we've examined before. As preposterous as the statement appears initially, my work as a psychologist has convinced me that the understanding about where we are in our awakening and what we have to work with in consciousness leads to our doing the best we can in any given moment no matter how poor or fine that may be. That statement is actually true. It is very relieving to take that in. We do not know what inner motivations, fears, belief systems, stress and pain may be at the base of anyone's behavior, including our own in entirety. We do not know where anyone is in their inner awakening to higher truth or what grade in this spiritual school any of us are currently struggling through. It is sometimes called POE, our point in evolution.

It became more and more clear to me that if I took these principles to inner levels of myself beyond simple intellectual understanding, the content of my lower mind would gradually improve in quality and diminish in quantity. There would be a great deal more stillness. I'd be more empty headed.

An idea extending from these principles is true and can be fun to work with. We toss it around at many of our gatherings. It is that much of what our minds dwell on is none of our business. I love that! If we choose to become quiet enough to really hear the content of our mental chatter, we will see that the belief system represented in the above paragraphs negates a number of our thoughts. Our only true work is to work on ourselves. Yes, we do have some additional obligations, but they are best carried out with Soul direction, not ego illusion.

So many of our thoughts do relate to judging in one form or another. Much of that judging is focused on what is none of our concern since we have totally insufficient information to assess the content of anyone's life or behavior, even those near and dear. And so I say again that we do not know what is best for anyone in the big picture of becoming enlightened. Thus, most of what we are exposed to is really none of our affair. It is just further temptation to judge and criticize or approve and applaud. We don't know; let it go. Choose peace instead.

Please recognize that I am not saying we never have a valid thought that produces useful fruit. Of course we do. So once we become more still and observant in our present moment, we can begin to more wisely separate the productive thinking from the non-productive. Our higher wisdom offers many good insights and direction but we are unlikely to hear that if we are focusing on our ego content.

And when our thoughts are drawn to what actually is our business, whether that be personal or professional, let us ask and listen for higher Soul guidance on how to proceed. Again only in relative stillness will we discern true understanding and knowledge to progress in our actions, to really effectively and perceptively make a difference.

When I returned from my retreat, much more in touch with my ongoing thoughts, I kept a log of the repetitive types of mental busyness that frequented my inner terrain. Then after a productive and quieting meditation, I would examine these thoughts for their truth and usefulness. There were some gems hidden in the mounds of worry and resentment, no doubt some Soul guidance sneaking in among the throngs of ego illusions. But most were extensions of my ego's desires and beliefs – very unworthy fare.

There are many simple practices that we can undertake that enable us to create some space between ourselves and the ongoing inner dialogue, practices that allow us to more frequently operate from the wisdom and love of our Higher Mind. Methods are readily available to become more empty headed. Several have been discussed in our various chapters and there are more to come. Again, Eckhart Tolle and Jon Kabat-Zinn are truly excellent teachers.

And flowing from their works is my favorite practice of focusing on my breath gently flowing in and out. We need a better point of attention than our normal ego fare to help us out. A truly empty head is a bit too demanding in reality. Focusing on our breath flow not only helps us to see the content of our thoughts, but additionally brings us into the present moment. We become more quiet and aware. We see things more clearly and calmly. We recognize that the one who is observing the thoughts is our inner self connected to our Higher Mind. The breath is an excellent doorway to higher truth, to greater peace and consciousness. There are also many short prayers, affirmations, and mantras that serve very well.

Our Higher Mind is Soul-connected, filled with the wisdom, perspective, and love of God. Our Higher Mind represents who we really are and is a source of greater wholeness and fulfillment. When we accomplish that ongoing connection, our mind is in a very quiet state of being. It is resting comfortably listening for direction and guidance from our Soul. What a lightened and enlightened state of consciousness that is. How unburdened we become. I believe it was Tolle who shared that stillness is the language of God and all else is a poor translation. How beautiful and true.

It is difficult to beat the equanimity of being empty headed. It is so relieving to let go of all that is none of our business. Try it out! Let's give ourselves the chance of experiencing a different state of consciousness, one that offers us the joy in life that we seek.

Chapter 17
Ego and the Car Dealership

Noticing when my thoughts, feelings, and actions are coming from my lower self evaluation of things is an ongoing effort. The realization that this ego analysis lacked any wisdom took awhile to develop. Gradually I began to notice after the ego-tainted fact that I had been operating from an unenlightened space. Then I started noticing my error in the midst of it all. And now, at least much of the time, I can see the ego analysis coming which gives me much more power to choose differently. I then choose from Soul understanding and perspective as much as I can pull it off. And choosing differently makes a terrific improvement in my quality of life and all my relationships. Does this remind you of our levels of serenity in Chapter 3?

The ego evaluation is usually based on self-interest and advancement and always on some level of fear. We might have to dig a bit to find the fear, but its hiding out in there somewhere. It may be fear of how people are thinking of us, fear of loss of what we have, fear of not being loved, fear of God, and surely you can fill in many blanks – there's plenty to discover. However, whatever the source of our current ego judgments of self, others, and situations may be, our daily peace is very much affected by how quickly we can identify and see through the ego analysis of things.

Again I say we are all so much more than the body and personality and we actually do have an inner Divine connection to our Soul that will guide us to wiser and more loving understanding of what's going on. That is surely the goal. As we nurture our spiritual awareness, we are more easily, quickly, and spontaneously in touch with that Divine wisdom within and act accordingly. Life then definitely takes a beautiful leap forward into greater joy and peace. We become much more healing in and to the world. We had a good talk about all of this in our last chapter and elsewhere.

So what about the car dealership you say? Well, in recent times it had become painfully apparent that I needed a newer car. My car had served me very well for many years, it never let me down and we had a great relationship, but all those molecules and atoms seemed tired and didn't want to go on. OK; I'm grateful for all the service it gave me. So I did some homework and then drove to a dealership that seemed to have a fairly new used vehicle that was just what I wanted.

I have grown very weary of thinking in any adversarial manner. I am not interested in expecting things to go wrong or people to be disappointing including myself. No doubt things sometimes occur in a seemingly undesirable manner but also no doubt my thinking and expectations have a powerful effect on every event in the flow of my life. So all the way up to the dealership I hold thoughts of goodwill and peace for this event.

My evaluation of a successful day at this point is how deep and loving my consciousness and its expression have been throughout those hours. So after forty years of spiritual practice my concern in this adventure was my state of consciousness rather than how good a deal I could argue my way into.

The transaction went very well. The car was great, the price after some civil and respectful discussion was satisfactory, and I was peaceful with the event and actually rather thrilled with my new car friend. And the guy who was sitting across from me was a little richer. Win-win!

However, here's where it got challenging to my ego. In the cubicle next to me, another woman was buying a car and not having quite as nice a time of it. Her salesperson held to the less pleasant methods of salesmanship and was dripping insincerity in his many compliments to her. To the best of my ability to perceive the situation, she was not being taken in by any of this and knew what she wanted and they, too, put together a satisfactory deal. She was now ready to exit the dealership with her new key in hand.

As a parting pat, the salesperson said to another person in front of her how she was so much smarter than both of them and that this fact had been clear throughout the interaction. The woman very gently turns to him, reached out her hand although not touching him, quietly laughed and says firmly yet gently "You can stop all that now; I've bought the car." And exited.

Now my first reaction in observing this interchange was to think "You go, girl! Speak for all us womenfolk". Times are not always easy for us in purchasing cars. I almost followed her out to give her a hug. Then I realized that my response was clearly coming from my ego. I was judging the situation and wanting to put him in his place. Foiled again!

Then I began thinking that I certainly cannot judge and condemn him since I know nothing of his situation, how many children he's trying to feed in this challenging economy, what he believes really are effective sales techniques (yikes, maybe those methods actually work a lot of the time), how evolved he is in connection to his own Soul, what stress and desperation he may or may not feel, and on it goes. So now I have backed off the poor guy and I'm sending him thoughts of acceptance and light.

Then I realize that I am still in the ego to some extent. I have not sought my inner guidance; I have not inquired of my Soul what the proper inner response is to this situation. I'm not saying it is easy to get all that right. Our daily spiritual nurturing is very important preparation for reaching for the inner wisdom at a moment's notice. But what a worthy goal! How our experience of life does change as we gradually develop this questioning and listening ability, this deep inner connection with Truth and Love.

Let us recall that one of our primary goals on the spiritual path is to cultivate a more peaceful and quiet and certainly less reactive mind. We are so accustomed to judging and criticizing an abundance of situations that are really none of our concern. Remember that "none of our business" stuff. We are so in a whirl of giving attention to the activities of the world around us, drawing conclusions and often dwelling upon them that the mind is usually in constant activity and not of a pleasant variety. And our inner personal reverie isn't all that uplifting most of the time either. We know all of this.

I have been posing a question to my wiser Self more frequently which is "is this mine?" Am I meant to pay attention to this situation, to interact with this individual in some way, is there something I can learn by pondering this? Am I to play some role here? Most of the time, thankfully, I am guided that it is not mine. It is just the ego searching for more distractions, busyness and criticisms. Sometimes there is a role awaiting me, if only to send loving energy, and I am guided to execute that role. We don't know until we ask.

So as I quiet myself while sitting in the dealership, I access the knowing that all my mind chatter about that other person's purchase and those involved was a waste of my peace and absolutely "not mine". Our ego mind is like a radar system searching our environment for something to pounce on and judge. When we come to value stillness, we will not want to dwell on irrelevant circumstances as much as possible. There really are wise ways of how to think about things or not to think about things at all. So much is "none of our business". Do we want inner peace or not?

Remember, we are never alone. Our Soul and its grand astuteness are always available for connection. Our Soul is in a state of Oneness with a myriad of more enlightened beings who have dedicated themselves to our awakening and the healing of the world. There is a vast dimension of advanced consciousness awaiting our access. Let's get on with the accessing.

I was mowing the lawn earlier today and found myself thinking of a variety of unnecessary topics. My mind was busy with little room for any stillness or inspiration. So I began one of my favorite little mantras that I use during tasks requiring no real thought. I said silently "quiet" on my inbreath and "mind" on my outbreath. And gradually the noise subsided which allowed room for peace and calm and any inner inspiration that might come my way. I do want that peace and am willing to work for it.

Chapter 18
The Waters Speak

*H*ere is another experience I would like to share with you and it feels like a fine way to conclude Part I of the book. It was very rich and meaningful to me although likely for full appreciation, you had to be there. It spoke of a concept I understand consciously. However, this experience had a power and depth that took a few others and me to a deeper knowing and appreciation. The concept concerned the life in all creation.

A few serious spiritual seekers had gathered for some shared inspiration and we had gotten onto the topic of what's happening in our oceans. Recently there had been so many reports of ocean creatures beaching themselves apparently due to illness and disorientation; we felt great compassion for their plight. We had read a good bit about the contamination of our waters that affected the ocean creatures as well as ourselves.

At this point I need to interject that for a few years now, there have been intermittent times when unexpected beings have spoken through me. When I feel that invitation coming my way, of course it is my decision as to whether I speak it aloud. However, since these events have taught me a great deal over time, I welcome the education this offers and value sharing these moments with others. An invitation was issued on this occasion and I accepted.

Now usually these experiences feel rather like 220 volts of electricity coming through a 110 volt vehicle (me). Always a bit of a stretch and some adjustment thereafter, all more than worth the information gained. But on this occasion it truly felt like 500 volts were coming through and I struggled to stay stable and properly aligned in the Light. As usual I was in one of my MAP connections and thus I had fine assistance with the process.

A powerful voice spoke in my mind. It felt mighty and ancient and huge and distinctly non-human. I repeated to our little group what I was hearing to the very best of my ability while feeling ever so deeply affected by the simplicity yet enormity of what it conveyed.

It went something like this: "We the Waters of the world wish to speak with you. We are grateful for the efforts being made to cleanse our substance; this is a worthy and needed effort. For time immemorial we have given of ourselves and nurtured all life on this planet as we are meant to do. Humanity, however, does not yet demonstrate a consciousness that allows an understanding that we are a Living Being; that we are Life as you are and that all Life must come together in connection and relationship and union. This is what will bring about our healing.

Look within your greatest depths and know that all Life is One and in that Oneness, quite sacred. Reach inside yourselves for that experience and wisdom. Let yourselves immerse in the energy of all Life and all will be well. That is the effort and resonance that will return us all to balance and our Divine connection. Without that, all other efforts will be limited in their effectiveness. Please heed our call."

The words I recall do no full justice to the experience. Perhaps many of you have enjoyed bliss at moments of peak awareness. Those few times that zenith has been mine have been filled with a peace and joy beyond anything I am able to describe. This connection is our destiny, our truth, our ultimate reality. And we never completely forget those incredible moments of viewing how things really are.

One of the folks present sagely responded that this was affecting her profoundly partly due to her realization that this call, this plea for recognition of being and union, was equally applicable to everything. It applied to all that is obviously alive and also to that which appears inanimate. I so loved her insight.

People have good-naturedly made fun of me for years because I experience a loving energy of oneness with all things. Not all the time yet but much of the time. My awareness, like yours, is still in progress. I don't believe my car or washing machine or favorite living room chair have an identity of themselves as being a car or washer or chair. Or maybe they do. But I know that the atoms, the molecules, all that make up the seeming inanimate objects are, of course, alive and do respond to energy. Science supports this today.

I offer love and gratitude to all living things. And I offer the same to all the energetic structures that make up the rest of our seemingly non-living world: furniture, clothes, cars, houses, all things. It feels wonderful and gives me much joy! I remember some years back the rather popular books by a Japanese scientist by the name of Masaru Emoto and his study of water and its energetic configurations. Those molecular configurations depend on what substances and energy the water is exposed to. His works are a marvelous read and a perfect example of how all life is affected by the quality of the many aspects of our environment. Offering love and gratitude to water produces the most beautiful and balanced cellular configurations. His books are filled with miraculous pictures and are a real mind bender, and an invitation to take all of this more seriously.

Sometimes when I sit alone late at night, I open to the energy that composes my entire environment--every molecule, every particle. I sink into a merger with everything present filling it all with my love and appreciation of how we have teamed up to get through this earthly journey together. Perhaps I sound rather crazy doing this. However those are special moments; all energy responds to my affectionate fusion and we rest in peaceful connection together – speaking of never being alone. Try it some time. It is ever so sweet. Just like the water, the entire world awaits our recognition and loving union.

However, many of us in our spiritual groups have worked with this kind of knowledge for years and we readily admit we do not always make the best use of it. When we examine what gets in our way, a number of answers appear. We too seldom nurture our spiritual lives and so easily forget these more ultimate realities. We are rushed and busy, our ego desires and attachments take precedence, and our priorities are all askew. But when we dig down and really listen to our own inner wisdom, we often find that most of these interferences and excuses stem from a devaluing of who we really are.

We have had many influences in our existence prodding us to dislike ourselves, feel great guilt, and believe that we are unworthy as beings. We overly identify who we are as our bodies and personalities, our pains and wounds, which are the most ephemeral and minute aspects of our Selves. If we cannot yet fully honor ourselves with respect and love and feel a wholeness within, it is no surprise that it is difficult for us to experience all of creation in the same manner.

Every moment you and I spend nurturing ourselves spiritually, we not only benefit ourselves but greater love flows out of us and affects all life in a nurturing and pure manner. This is surely one of the central motivations I feel for sharing these thoughts with you. We are all invited and indeed strongly requested to change our priorities and reach for the highest and best of who and what we are. We must all support one another in moving forward toward that awakening into true spiritual union and bliss.

Will you join me in the effort and adventure? Your answer to that and what flows from that answer are well worth serious inner contemplation. As we gradually learn to live in a state of pure love and light, all things will be benefited - all oceans, all seeming inanimate things, all humans, all nature, and all life. Our energies pervade all. We are all One.

Chapter 19
Introduction to Part II
So what do we do Now?

*O*ur own spiritual intentions combined with our efforts are paramount to our awakening process and the pace it proceeds. We might ask ourselves at this point "What does my life mean to me?", "What are my primary goals?", "Where am I spiritually?", and "How much focus do I wish to place on moving ahead in my awakening?" Quiet inner reflection is needed to aid us in clarifying what we truly want for ourselves and how much we wish to participate in the healing of our world and all within it.

My answer to those questions certainly varied with the stage of life I was in. How much time I could devote to spiritual practice and what that meant to me has surely had its ups and downs. My life and perhaps yours as well has been a very busy affair, often filled with worthy activities and sometimes sidetracked with meaningless and unworthy pursuits. I recall my delight when I was exposed to meditation methods that were designed to be used during any active part of my day. Breath work was exceedingly helpful in that it can be combined with almost any activity if we just remember to do it. More of this is coming up very soon.

Through the decades there have been a wondrous variety of sacred methods that have accelerated my dawning awakening. The movement forward is ongoing and every piece of added understanding and ability to connect with my own Soul has been and is of great value. They add to my serenity and contentedness. They increase my clarity of mind and wholeness of heart. This allows me to be a better servant to higher needs and the will of God. I cannot too strongly recommend that each of us finds what practices are right for us at this point in our lives and pursue them with diligence and joy.

Part II of this book is about methods and practices for moving on spiritually. Part I had some goodies of that nature here and there but now we move into chapters solely dedicated to offering us many options to realize who we really are and how to live in that peace and fulfillment. A few tried and true spiritual devotees, very dear friends of mine, have graciously added information and testimonials at various points and they are valuable material offering additional points of view.

So off we go! Experiment, seek guidance, and contemplate what might be right for your next step. Do one; do them all! However, do so with a lightness of heart unburdened with weighty expectations and just observe how it flows for you. Bring patience, persistence and calm to the process as much as you are able. And remember, we are never alone in our efforts and the Universe well utilizes every moment we spend in such pursuit and generosity. We do it for us all.

Chapter 20
Our Many Forms of
Spiritual Practice

*T*his is a great first chapter for this section since it is an overview of a number of spiritual practices, our topic for Part II. Many of us are becoming more involved in enhancing our connection with our Higher Self, reaching for the peace and joy that it brings. Many of us wish to be a more active force in uplifting our fellow humans. When we consciously make the decision to work toward higher realization on a daily basis, our journey does indeed accelerate. And you and I, those around us, and the world in general are benefited.

We may feel we are doing this only for our own advancement but that is never the case. Consciousness is contagious as we've discussed. Our energy projects out from ourselves and connects with other similar energies forming a positive or negative and unseen cloud-like affair that influences the space of others. What quality of awareness and energy do we project and share? It is our minute-by-minute perspective, thoughts, and feelings that determine this. Those choices will be more enlightened if we nurture our Soul connection through these practices. So let's review some of the forms that many individuals have found valuable.

A primary activity supporting spiritual advancement is service to others. True spiritual service can be in the form of our energy projected or a thought, word, or deed offered from a sense of love, with no self-gain or fear or "should" involved. It is best chosen and accomplished, when possible and practical, after we have quieted ourselves and sought guidance on what is ours to do. Otherwise, our service may be misplaced. Our personal resources such as love, time, and money are given us to share wisely. The joy and compassion that we gain through service moves us forward in Spirit more rapidly. So it is ever so wise to expand our vision of the many forms service does take and what state of mind we are best in while offering it.

I'm going to insert here a short quote from my dear friend Dr. Rusty Stephens' excellent work, *Dialogues With The Holy Spirit*, which offers a beautiful section on service coming from a very high place. This book has just come out in 2011 and is available on Amazon. I think you will find it inspiring as I did. The Wisdom Teachings refers to the Bailey works.

> The Wisdom Teachings state that three activities are requisite to Spiritual growth. They are meditation, study and service.
>
> The greatest of these is service. By starting with the nearest brother and taking his need as the measure of your response, you begin to break old patterns of the separated self. Service puts you into a new perspective as you cannot help but see your brother in new

ways. In this sense your brother is your teacher and perfect Spiritual partner for he brings the lesson you are in need of. His very presence allows you the opportunity for the growth that you seek. His need is the match for your own. He is your gift from God as you are his.

True service, entered into from the heart, and with no motive but that to serve, not only allows you to embrace the unity of all things; it requires you to do so. It is one of the strongest opponents of the little ego. True service requires a shift in consciousness to higher levels and away from the focus on the indulgences of the lower self; in this sense, true service gets you out of yourself.

I have certainly found that to be true. Service is always an excellent opportunity to examine our deeper motives for what we do. Who is the service really for? One of our study group members was sharing that she found herself "serving" while realizing it was mostly for her own benefit. She couldn't further tolerate the feelings within herself which were generated by the suffering she was seeing. And she felt like a finer person having helped the individual. So surely a productive spiritual practice aided by service is examining our true motives for our behaviors. Most often our actions are a mixture of motives. Seeing our ego involvement in a service does not mean we don't carry out our plans. We just remain aware of our various reasons for involvement. Then two worthy things occur at once.

Our chapter coming up on "Radiatory Service" will expand our appreciation that service can simply be a loving and healing thought sent into the world. For that matter any peaceful and caring moment with no effort for anything being sent anywhere continues to radiate out into the environment as well. Our state of mind is a service or often not so. Let us remember that excellent world service can be offered from our own homes.

What about spiritual study? To spend regular amounts of time focusing our thoughts on spiritual perspectives lightens our load and brings wisdom into our daily life. The most common form of study is to read and reflect on spiritually-oriented material, be it one of the bibles of the world, *A Course In Miracles*, or any of the voluminous inspiring materials available today.

The challenge is to select that which fits where we are and where we want to go which requires inner discrimination. Even ten minutes a day spent studying and applying our understanding can transform our lives.

Let us not forget "contemplative meditation" which too is a form of study. We may choose any spiritual thought, passage, question, or concept and quietly and pensively open our minds to greater understanding about it. We would wisely ask for higher guidance for deeper comprehension at such moments. It is a combination of study and meditation and can be ever so productive. Those moments bring greater inner stillness as well as further wisdom.

Now we move on to prayer. No doubt talking to Higher Power, by whatever name, is a tremendous solace to many. However, much of our prayer comes from a belief that we know what is best for ourselves and others. Some prayer turns into a personal wish list with very little higher guidance and wisdom playing a role. We've all been there, especially at traumatic times.

As we've discussed, much religious material reminds us that we are here in this human journey only to awaken in spirit and unite with God. That being so, we do not know what experiences in life best support that awakening. The most difficult give us the opportunity for the quickest advancement. We are told that our journey here is "perfect and safe". It is not perfectly comfortable or catering to our ego desires, but perfect for speeding our progress. These understandings assist the form of my prayers.

I bring up Shakti Gawain again and, to my recall, she mentioned decades ago how wise it is to end every prayer with a statement something like "May this or something greater still in Divine Wisdom take place". I'm sure this isn't a direct quote but the concept is accurate and a super principle. "Thy Will be done." It is really tough to surrender in these ways; our ego pulls at us strongly. We do the best we can with the help of our Soul.

Today we recognize more than ever that prayer is powerful. Research has proven this to be true. We may be able to affect someone's condition through prayer although that may not be that person's best outcome. They may be delayed in their journey; maybe this illness offers a learning opportunity. Thus we have the common expression "Be careful what you pray for because you might get it". That applies to prayers for ourselves and others. Seeking guidance for proper prayer is always a win. Wisdom is needed. Many of us stay with the simple prayer that we or others be assisted in making the right decisions in our challenges. We ask that we be given the wisdom, courage, patience, and love to get through what is necessary. This is indeed a safe and sage request!

Another angle on prayer is that it is our deepest desire in a given situation that is responded to by Divine

Beings, often called the "sponsoring thought". I think Neale Donald Walsch, in his very successful series of books beginning with *Conversations With God*, may have coined that very useful phrase. So if our words pray for success but we hold a deep fear of success within, it is not the words that will rule. Thus many people feel their prayers are not answered. We are often unaware of what our deepest sponsoring thoughts actually are. We're often a bundle of mixed desires and fears.

Often prayers are answered in ways we don't recognize. Sometimes increased inner knowing and fortitude is our answer. Right now a dear friend of mine is very ill as a result of an accident. (Yes, I do have many, many dear friends.) It is very challenging for me to not fall into the ego prayer for him to be well again in the physical sense. But I just can't do that. I am sending him light and love and courage to deal with what his Soul knows is his finest outcome. It is clear that our prayer evolves in its form as we advance in our spiritual understanding.

Often people get in touch with me requesting I pray for a specific outcome for something they or a loved one is going through. I use to tell them what I pray for as I prayed in the example above, and unfortunately that has occasionally been distasteful to some, which I certainly do understand and regret. Sometimes they have said "Well, just skip it then". It is very difficult for all of us to really come to believe we do not know what lies in anyone's ultimate finest wellbeing. Very challenging! At this point I just pray for them in the highest sense knowing that is all to the finest good and skip the conversation on details.

Whatever form of prayer feels right to you, it's a great idea to not only share your thoughts and feelings with our Source but also allow for quiet, reflective time to perhaps sense the wisdom that may come to you. When our prayer time also includes a time of listening and deep inner quiet, it becomes much more productive.

How about spiritual journaling? Many of us take a few minutes daily to review, sometimes in written form, what our goals are and how we are doing in living our value system. At times included in this is a checksheet listing our hopes and assigning a 1 to 5 scale for success for the day. That's a little too detailed and compulsive for most but some folks really value this specificity. In whatever form, spiritual journaling is an excellent reminder of what we are striving to attain; and reviewed daily, it increases our effectiveness in living. If we can abstain from guilt and self-denigration when not achieving our goals, and instead ask Heavenly Help to support us as we try to do better, journaling is a much more peaceful process. The path is a lengthy one and our errors teach us more than our successes in many cases. Errors are expected for growth.

Several friends use their spiritual journal twice daily as I have at times. They look it over in the morning as a reminder of what they are aiming for that day and before bed to reflect on and write about how the day went. If we are wise enough to not expect perfect success each day, this can be a rewarding strategy for moving forward. It certainly demonstrates our genuine aspiration to greater attainment.

Mini-reminders of love and truth can be scattered throughout our day. Some examples are setting our phone or watch to beep hourly and when it sounds, taking a minute for centering and inspiration. Having post-it notes within our normal viewing area at work, home, or in the car to remind us of our spiritual goals or God's love is uplifting.

Taking our driving time for prayer or a spiritual CD also works well to readjust our perspective. We waste a great deal of driving time which can often be used to uplift ourselves and perhaps those with us. A few of my friends with children play very calming and harmonious music while driving and definitely think it influences the children's behavior for the better. Some of us have chosen inspiring screensavers. I like to do housework (well, I don't actually like to do housework) with an inspiring CD playing through my headphones. Eckhart Tolle's *"A New Earth"* is one of my favorites; I listen to it over and over again always hearing something I didn't really get before.

Some of our group members have committed to using bathroom or restroom visits to relax the body and mind for a moment and reach for higher energy as I've mentioned before – my "john meditation" – a great space for a touch of reflection. Any mechanical activities, showering, cooking, doing dishes, mowing the lawn, can be used to deepen and expand our breaths and perhaps to repeat a relaxing phrase of our choice. Try making a habit of taking a few deep breaths releasing tensions and drawing in Soul love in the midst of all activities. We are very powerful in choosing what state of consciousness we wish to live in and share with others. Let us not consider ourselves to be the victims in our day but rather the creators of our state of being.

Speaking of breathing, in the East there is an advanced science of "pranayama", the science of breath. Many of these techniques have been validated by Western science. There are various forms of breath control that can quickly energize or relax or awaken us to higher consciousness. Dr. Andrew Weil, M.D. offers us excellent training in these simple and very doable techniques.

His CD "Breathing – The Master Key to Self-Healing" is excellent and can be found as part of his self-healing series at www.soundstrue.com. I've already mentioned Dr. Jon Kabat-Zinn and Eckhart Tolle in this regard. Lots of sources of breath training are available. Many of us are surprised by the power of these simple techniques. I have used them with great success and been impressed with the results for years.

Working with a meaningful phrase has power as well. We may choose a question to frequently repeat that refocuses our awareness. A beautiful and recently popular one is "What would Jesus do?" Another suggestion would be "Is this who I really am?" And one of my favorites is from *Conversations With God* - "What would love do now?" These, sincerely stated, will always advance our thought and behavior and bring greater peace. A number of my friends use phrases from the Psalms or a spiritual book that really touches them. The possibilities are infinite but the choice should fit us; they should speak to our heart.

Working on our Forgiveness skills is challenging yet very rewarding. That surely is another spiritual practice producing a true change of mind when accomplished on any occasion. Forgiveness here is defined by *A Course In Miracles'* perspective which is that there is never any occurrence requiring our Forgiveness; nothing takes place that does not have an underlying purpose, a possible positive outcome. That's a concept that most of us balk at with intensity which is why I review it here a bit again in addition to our other chapter on the topic.

As we realize that everything that happens has meaning and opportunity for Soul expansion and that at that Soul level we have agreed to the various experiences and circumstances of our lives, it becomes much easier to consider such a seeming far-fetched idea. Forgiveness does not mean allowing poor behavior to continue, our own or others. Rather it is coming closer to a place of peace within and seeking Higher Guidance on how to experience true Forgiveness and what to do about the situation at hand.

Sometimes the answer is to take wise and decisive action; sometimes not. Often when I calm down and hear the voice of my Soul, I see that I have not heard or seen the occurrence accurately. I was once famous for thinking something was about me when it was not and being too sensitive when others meant nothing personal. This was simply a reflection of my own lack of complete self-Forgiveness which made me vulnerable to guilt and feelings of unworthiness. That wound then could easily be touched by others. Always more work to do but worth it.

Another great spiritual practice is working on giving up our constant judgments. If you have done much meditation, you will be well aware that the mind is filled with judging most everything. Non-judgment entails not condemning ourselves or others and never putting anyone out of our hearts. I think that is expressed in such statements as "We dislike, perhaps reject and correct, the behavior, but we value the human being". Yes, we remain aware and responsible for our own inner and outer behavior. And, yes, we surely make many daily assessments of what to embrace or reject.

However, we are capable of doing this from a mind space of respect and care, and from that calmer stance we are able to assess the situation more wisely. If we are acting from a place of negative emotion, our best assessment and action will not come about. Perhaps our most helpful self-test for whether we are judging and condemning is noticing when we are responding with some form of negative emotion, outwardly demonstrated or not. When do we discipline our children or grandchildren the best and most effectively? It is when we are calm and centered and handling the situation through wisdom. We all know that, right? All the material in this section is a useful review of the concepts examined earlier. We need to analyze these ideas again and again. What do they mean for us?

When negative emotion is present, we are judging something or someone in the situation. That certainly shows us how often we are condemning since we know how frequently we experience negative feelings. Even if we are just feeling very stressed, at some level we have decided that things should not be as they are. How do we know? I imagine this all sounds very lofty but even managing a little of this here and there allows us much more peace of mind and better relationships. And if our negative feelings teach us something about what needs to be altered, inside or outside of ourselves, then through higher guidance take action on this with a calmer and more understanding heart.

Whatever our perspective is on these valued ways of viewing life, it is wise to pause and be sure to daily apply the parts that make sense to us. We, ourselves, benefit the most from living these values; we are the ones who flow through our day less burdened. So whether we journal or have daily reminders placed throughout our environment or choose to Forgive and judge less, let us drop back to our chosen practices.

No matter what our spiritual goals may be, they will be aided in accomplishment if we ask for help from our own Soul, Higher Power, or whatever more advanced beings we are drawn to and depend upon. Throughout the day whenever we are confronted with difficult decisions and moments that require our healing love and good judgment, let us learn to reach for the wisdom of God. We will always gain by doing so but to maximize our capacity to perceive God's will, some purification is most helpful. It is unlikely we will perceive Higher Purpose when our egos are clamoring to have things our own way. The more we can surrender to what our journey entails, the better are our chances of knowing just what that is. Let's slow down, ask for help, and quietly listen. That is a purer approach. And surely it is a good spiritual practice.

This may sound somewhat passive at first glance; its not. Perhaps our journey presently requires learning to be more assertive or more involved. Perhaps it requires our being more relaxed about making things happen. Perhaps it changes from situation to situation. Only in our inner quiet reflection can we know what will serve ourselves and others in the finest way in a given moment.

Refining our ability to quiet our minds and give up our ego desires is paramount. Practice is very much required. If we are not developing this habit regularly, when we need guidance the most, we will neither ask nor listen. This is true for all of the practices herein. If we gradually work with any of these until they become an integrated part of our day and consciousness, then they will be in place when we need them, when the true crises are in our face.

Let's discuss the practice of visualization. In truth we are forming pictures in our minds all the time in response to whatever thoughts we are entertaining. Images of what we think will happen or what we want to happen are powerful especially if they are persistent. It is said that potent, positive visualization is an essential

tool on our path of becoming accomplished disciples of
the Light. Once we begin to recognize the importance of
this ability and the discipline to not entertain negative
images, we are on our way to greater effectiveness for
good.

Until that time, most of us visualize negative
situations all too frequently. I recall a time that was very
enlightening to me and much needed. A good friend had
fallen on difficult times and succumbed to an excessive
use of alcohol and drugs to ease his woes. I was very
concerned about him and caught myself thinking of him
all too often yielding to his temptations. Then I recalled
the teaching that the energy sent from me through that
unintentional visualization was adversely affecting him. I
needed to imagine him strong and more able to cope with
his troubles and addictions. I realized I was contributing
to his problems by not controlling my concerns and the
content of my own mind. I have been very watchful of
my inner scenes since then. With the best of intentions,
it is easy for any of us to drop into imagining negative
scenarios which just worsen the situation.

I'm reminded of many stories shared with me by
persons in great difficulty or someone close to a person
who is. They spend a few minutes a day envisioning
light, love, strength and wisdom going to the individual
(or themselves) with some very fine results taking place.
Those of us who have come to really accept that we don't
know the specifics of what should happen to anyone are
watchful as to what we are envisioning. Not only is that a
gift to the recipient but is excellent practice in honing our
ability to concentrate. Most of us do not concentrate well
for any sustained period of time. Meditation really helps
with that. Being able to visualize wisely and powerfully
is definitely a required skill on the path. There are many

books available today on visualization; teaching and training are plentiful. We must keep in mind, however, that inner Soul discrimination should illuminate just what we visualize. We are advised to reach for the finest of wisdom and not just attempt to fulfill ego desires.

One of my wisest and most accomplished friends, Patricia, has suggested I include a few references here that she has found quite valuable. Visualization is one of her many specialties. She finds the CDs of Belleruth Naparstek a wealth of information and training for the body, mind, and spirit. These can be found at www. healthjourneys.com. Her favorite books on this topic are *Cell-Level Healing, the Bridge from Soul to Cell* by Joyce Whiteley Hawks, Ph.D. which is a testimony to visual imagery and its power in the healing process. It can be obtained through Amazon. And *The Reconnection, Heal Others, Heal Yourself* by Dr. Eric Pearl combines the use of visual imagery and sound healing and can be found at www.hayhouse.com or 800-654-5126. Helpful resources truly are readily available these days.

Our work in this chapter would surely not be complete without further comments on healing ourselves of what ails us physically, emotionally, and mentally. All that we might do to bring greater wholeness to ourselves, from meditation to working with a wholistic physician or healer, is work that allows us to be finer servants in healing the world as well as ourselves. And certainly that includes the product of any spiritual practice we embrace; they all bring greater wellness and wholeness to our entire being.

Many books have been written on these various topics. Never underestimate the value of becoming more sound of body, mind, and spirit and how that affects many others as well. Chapter 26 centers on a process of healing our entire being called MAP which I have mentioned many times and may interest some of you. It has certainly proven to be an extremely valuable part of my spiritual practice and healing in the last twenty years. Chapter 32 relates to self-healing as well.

Another practice that a number of our group members found value in is from a book by Brandon Bays entitled *The Journey*. Her experiences and assistance to others have produced what is called "the Journey Process" which can be done alone or, better yet, with someone close or a mental health professional. The gist of it is that we all have many levels of emotion connected to any distressful event or memory. Her process teaches us to move down through these levels going deeper into our psyche. This has a final product for many of producing significant insight and healing and allows us to drop into a purer Soul space of greater peace and fulfillment.

This is a distant and worthy cousin to Gordon Davidson's work mentioned in several places in these pages which also represents a personal method to bring healing to the pains and wounds lodged in our subconscious. These efforts and processes can well be part of a wholistic spiritual movement forward and well worth our investigation. Healing ourselves is a spiritual practice of much importance.

Exciting methodologies of the 21st Century are coming to our attention. Two very promising aspects of this are the spiritual and healing effects of both sound and light. Science is investigating the healing and harmful aspects of both and more information and resulting technologies are coming our way annually. Further claims are made as to the healing applications of both of these resources. I am not proficient in this knowledge but I am aware enough of what seems to be developing to perhaps pique interest. The internet being what it is, we have no trouble looking for further information on what calls to us.

A very simple and inexpensive example of beneficial and uplifting sound is a CD that our groups have found impactful to higher consciousness. It is called "Holy Harmony" by Jonathan Goldman with Sarah Benson. They utilize tuning forks said to represent the complete healing codes of the Christian Bible combined with a magnificent chant of an ancient name for the Christ. It is deeply compelling and transforming to listen to. You can check it out at www.healingsounds.com or 800–246–9764. I use it in all of my workshops. My understanding is that there are many such diverse examples of this type of stimulation available today for our examination.

We cannot discuss these beneficial functions of sound without alerting ourselves to the many harmful sounds surrounding us in many environments. As far back as the seventies, there were scientific studies done with plant activity and various forms of music. As I recall plants progressed beautifully with classical music being played and actually died with hard rock. But all of us know of current sounds and settings that we experience as detrimental to our consciousness. So part of our spiritual practice is remaining aware of how our inner and outer environment influences our state of health, mind and Spirit.

My friend, Pat, is well educated in the arena of light and sound as well as visualization and has loaned me a rather advanced technology. It is a machine called Nova Pro 100 that offers a wide array of sounds and light frequencies. Its binaural beats and pitch and frequency choices are many, taking us into relaxation, meditation, sleep, energizing states, and more. The sounds joined with light frequencies are attuned to our particular goals, and come to us through special glasses. I must say I have been impressed as to its various effects. It is costly but for those who wish to speed up their awakening processes through technology, it's a goody. I don't believe it does anything we cannot do with our own minds through training and practice but lots of folks value the short cut. It can be investigated at www. photosonix.com.

Let me assure you again that no one urges me to mention the various authors and practices I bring up in this book other than a few friends. These are simply methods or technologies that have been brought to my attention and been tested by me and folks in our various groups. I'm sure there are loads of helpful materials out there about which I've heard nothing.

And now to the last practice we'll get into here–seeing the Divine Eternal Self in us all. We are all equally Divine Souls in our true identity, although not all equally demonstrating that Divinity in the outer world as yet. Consciously look into another's eyes and recognize their spiritual essence. Although most certainly we do better at this if we've been practicing on the folks we love and have no contention with. That is a starting point. Better yet, start with ourselves, although that can be fraught with tough insights.

Recognize the Higher Self that is the center of your being. Tell yourself that you love yourself unequivocally. Don't be taken in by the personality and body. Look into the mirror each day, look deeply into your own eyes, and work your way through the layers of rejection and feelings of unworthiness. Often before we reach that feeling of acceptance and love, we may notice our resistance looking back at us. We often automatically reflect on all the physical, emotional, and mental aspects of ourselves that we do not like.

That in itself is valuable in that we need to face what we have tried to deny or reject so that we can work on releasing those judgments causing the rejection. A tall order, but each step forward to self-acceptance and love lightens our burdens and makes each day more joyful. Don't be taken in by your exterior either; that is just temporary housing. This is a difficult exercise and takes time to develop. The result is a sense of love and union with all; it takes place first with ourselves, then others, and then all creation.

My hope is that something in this chapter may attract you; something may seem worthy of a good try. Pick out what feels right and give it a shot. Many of them work together. Let us not be saddened when we don't reach our goals. Let's have some fun with it.

And please consider not getting preachy about all this with others. It is good practice to listen within quietly for when it is time to share some of this with those around us. That's when it will count. And very often being a model of it is much more powerful.

More detail lies in the chapters ahead. And if you are wondering why meditation wasn't mentioned in this chapter, it is because loads of information on that finest of practices lies in the next chapter.

Chapter 21
Meditation: Our
Royal Road Home

*N*ever enough could be said about the many benefits of meditation and how very important it is to our realizing all we can be and are. Meditation offers us greater relaxation and contentment in our lives. It is becoming increasingly popular among many people of all walks of life as well as those in the medical arena. It is effective in improving the well-being of the body and mind as well as a deepening of our spirituality.

With the many forms of meditation easily accessible today, there is some type of meditation which can be mastered and put to good use by any interested person. That certainly includes you if you are not already involved in this practice. With dedication and repetition we can harness the power of our own mind. In other words, you and I are quite capable of taking charge of how we feel and what we share through a few minutes of effort each day.

Meditation might well be defined as an exercise designed to bring stillness and quiet to our normal mental busyness. We gradually learn to simply observe our thoughts and feelings and not become entangled in them. We become more adept at releasing distractions and moving back to our meditative technique. This brings about an inner centeredness and repose that allows a balancing and healing for our entire being. Meditation produces a strengthening of our connection to our higher mind as physical exercise produces a strengthening of our body. We become the master of our own mental activity. And we all know what an aggravation our present mental activity can be. It takes time but is worth every moment of endeavor.

Many treasure meditation since it goes beyond having any particular religious or spiritual belief system or, in fact, having none at all. It is a method anyone can use with profit. *A Course in Miracles* espouses the idea that it is impossible for everyone in the world to agree on religious beliefs. Rather what is possible, even imperative, is that everyone have the experience of the great love of God for one and all as I've mentioned before. Meditation is a very potent path to that experience which heals many deep wounds. We are invited to go beyond thought into the realm of pure awareness where resting in higher realization gives us what we truly seek. We experience God's unconditional love.

I recall one meditation teacher of years ago saying we are not responsible for every thought that enters our mind during meditation or any other time. We are only responsible for those we embrace. Remember that? This is a memorable truth. It's a wondrous mental power to be able to simply witness our thoughts come and go without clinging or judgment, without holding onto them. We gradually come to know that who we are is not our thoughts and feelings but so much more than that. We identify with our lower mind content less and less. That ability takes awhile to develop and is by far worth every minute we put into it. We gradually come to experience our own spiritual aliveness within, our pure being, and all else pales.

An impressive amount of research has been published in the last thirty years supporting the daily practice of meditation. For example, one study discussed the health benefits garnered by 2000 US meditators as compared to an equal number of non-meditators. The findings for those who meditated included a reduction in heart disease and diseases of the nervous system, a reduction in tumors of all types, and a reduction in all infectious diseases.

A number of insurance companies around the world are now offering premium reductions to those who regularly practice meditation techniques. There have been many reports of lowered muscle tension, reduced pain, and more relaxed brainwave patterns reflecting a calm state of mind. The reduced pain has brought about meditation's use in many pain clinics. Increased immune functioning allows for greater resilience against illnesses of many varieties.

Through the years there has been research indicating that meditation leads to reduced blood pressure, cholesterol levels, stress hormones, and reduced use of addictive substances. Also discussed were improvements in many psychological conditions such as anxiety, depression, nervousness, and aggression and increases in self-confidence.

Psychological gains are common. Our increased sense of well-being and peace allow for better concentration, self-discipline, efficiency, and can even improve our relationships with others. In being more centered and less defensive, we can become better listeners and communicators and be generally more sensitive and caring. We learn to see beyond the foibles of our personalities to our Divine Eternal Selves. Wise Forgiveness and action take the place of ego reactivity.

Cognitive improvement of various kinds has been researched as well. Diverse types of useful thinking as well as increases in memory and quicker recognition may well result depending on what type of meditation we are practicing.

Spiritually speaking, many individuals meditate to align with Higher Reality known by so very many titles. As we quiet, the wisdom of our inner being is more accessible. Often the purpose and direction in our lives becomes clearer. Many friends have commented that they feel a much greater kinship with all human beings and actually all of life.

I'll share here a little of my own journey with meditation. I didn't know any of the above information in the sixties when I felt immensely stressed and fatigued. School, work, relationships, dealing with my own neuroses and a recent divorce – all of this felt like very demanding stuff. And then the Beatles began meditating under the tutelage of Maharishi Mahesh Yogi who offered Transcendental Meditation to one and all. I was a little slow to get on the bandwagon. It cost money which I didn't have. And my hours already were filled to the minute.

However, I was living in the Washington, D.C. area at the time and it became quite trendy to meditate. My friends were telling me it would assist my plight greatly. I said no, absolutely no time available. They said that if I did it as suggested, it would save me time. I would become more centered and calm. I wouldn't waste time looking for my keys or reading my graduate school materials over and over because my mind wasn't present when I read them the first time. They believed my relationships (including the one with myself which was definitely shaky) would really smooth out as I became less reactive and sensitive. So I began saving my pennies.

They were right! Who knew?? Well, I guess they did having been doing it themselves. And since I had to pay for it with money I really couldn't spare, I began doing it quite consciously and consistently, twice a day just as I was instructed. Ah, the motivational power of money! And within weeks I could really begin to feel a difference. I was calming down. My mind was much clearer. I could find my keys; I even remembered to buy cat food. My studies took me much less time because my focus had really improved. I was more energetic.

Much more fitted into my day comfortably because I wasn't such a basket case. My evenings were much more productive since I did one of my meditations after work. It was like a new start to the day once I got the hang of it. Super! I had no interest in the spiritual angle of it yet. I just wanted some sanity. Well, it did all it was touted to do – physically, mentally, emotionally, and, within about six months, spiritually as well.

After those first few months I began to feel a more on-going connection with Spirit that I had sought for years. My Soul became a reality for me. I felt something of my inner life and Spirit. My love and appreciation for who we all are began to bud. So I stuck with this practice for several years.

I even went so far as to join the first American class of Maharishi's Siddhi Program in the seventies. This was a long-term, intermittent training in siddhis, which is the Sanskrit word for spiritual powers. That was almost forty years ago. Some of you folks around my age might remember the bad press we all received. Indeed, much fun was made of it all, and understandably so. We were the hoppers. Part of the program was designed to teach us to levitate. I was in the first class to complete the program in this country and, believe it or not, we did get off the ground, but little hovering commenced I can assure you. We hopped rather high actually but no actual levitation took place. I heard the Europeans did much better.

However, what was really impressive about it for me was the state of consciousness I would touch upon in the midst of a hop. I'm not even going to try to describe it here; I don't know how. I will say that at that moment of brief flight I knew and understood things about the Universe that I certainly never knew before and could barely recall in detail thereafter. It was my first deep experience of just how profound, intricate, and mysterious Creation really is. That's the part of that training that I will never forget and will forever be grateful for. That truly changed me.

Actually part of what induced me to continue taking spiritual training much more seriously was a journey I undertook a few years before then. After completing my Ph.D., I worked for a year saving all the money I could and then bought a van. An old love of mine in the commune I lived in helped me put in flooring and shelves. He was of great assistance as he was so much looking forward to my absence. I gave myself a giant present. I took a year off, lived in the van, and traveled alone throughout the United States, part of Canada and part of Mexico working when needed. Ah, those were the trusting days.

I did and saw many worthy things but chief among them was visiting spiritual retreats, monasteries and teachers. It was a very rich year for me. It seemed like my entire nervous system shifted and I was in a deeply quiet and aware state that I had not maintained for very long before that time; actually that had only taken place in meditative states. I was exposed to so many wise beings and holy places and energies. A couple of years after this trip was when I did the training described above.

Then a couple more years went by and I had the finest of fortunes to hear about a very great spiritual teacher visiting in the state of New York. I couldn't wait to get to South Fallsburg where His beautiful ashram was being formed. Every hope and expectation was fulfilled. Swami Muktananda, Head of the Siddha Yoga Foundation at that time, was by far the most advanced being I had ever been exposed to and I had been around a few by then. He, His teachings, His Shakti (in a sense that means power to awaken us), and his successor, Gurumayi, are discussed beautifully by a deeply sincere and accomplished Siddha Yoga devotee in the following chapter. Oh, by the way, I suppose some of you know that Gurumayi was the teacher featured in the film with Julia Roberts entitled "Eat, Pray, and Love".

My meditation and daily consciousness took a most appreciated spurt of growth through those years of being around Baba, as Swami Muktananda was affectionately called. Our time spent in the ashram was disciplined and packed with inspiring meditation and chanting, challenging and expanding teachings, and an increased dedication to service. The energy emanating from this very great Being lifted us all to higher inspiration and action. Great calm and centeredness would enter our minds as well as times of turmoil as the energy began to bring our wounds to the surface for healing. It reminds me now of Eckhart Tolle's quote in his book, *A New*

Earth – "Stillness is the language of God; all else is a poor translation". I love repeating that although there is no way to convey the truth of it in words; it must be experienced.

Now back to more formal information on meditation. There are many forms and the short and inexpensive book, *How to Meditate* by Dr. Lawrence LeShan, is excellent in regard to types of meditation and other relevant information. That book has been around awhile but still is quite valued for its breadth of practices. Any method you might choose needs to be practiced consistently for several weeks before you can assess how well it will serve your needs.

Before each meditation session it is very wise to do a minimum of two or three minutes of slow, even, deep breathing, releasing all tensions of the body and mind with each breath. If you have come across the alternate nostril breath practice, that is an excellent entry into shifting your consciousness at the beginning of a meditation. Also the relaxing breath taught by Dr. Andrew Weil is especially beneficial and can save much time in settling down to a good meditation. A few minutes spent in breath work reaps excellent rewards during the meditation itself; you'll have much better focus. The following are two useful methods of meditation for those just starting out.

After seating yourself comfortably and privately, closing your eyes, and spending a few minutes relaxing through the breath, then release the breath focus and begin to repetitively, silently, and gently repeat the phrase "I am relaxing into peace." Focus on the feeling and meaning of the words, and with each repetition release into a deeper experience of quiet and peace of body and mind. It becomes a deeper experience with every practice session and increased ability to remain focused. After fifteen or twenty minutes, release the phrase, sit quietly for another minute or two to allow your nervous system to adjust and then slowly open your eyes. Notice the change that you have created, recognize the power you have to fashion your state of mind, and go on with your day.

A second beginning method is similar but adds ongoing breath work. After doing the initial breath as above just to calm yourself, begin to focus your attention on the experience of your breath flowing in and out of your body. Make no effort to change its rhythm or depth. Just notice quietly. Feel the slight movement of your abdomen. Then you might add any peaceful or healing word or phrase to correspond with the breath, stated silently within. You might say "I am" on the in breath and "letting go" on the out breath. Or you might form your own words for this method or the first one above. Pay attention to their impact.

Perhaps a single word like "love" or "quiet" might well suffice. Or you might have heard of a simple Sanskrit mantra that really appealed to you. Many people use the ever powerful mantra "OM". Some folks gently count their breaths from one to ten and then start again. It is humbling how seldom beginners reach ten. That was surely true for me.

As my years of teaching meditation have gone by, it's become clear to me that a "busy" meditation for beginners can be very helpful. That may sound strange. However, when we are first working at quieting and disengaging from our thoughts, we really need other more uplifting activities to put in their place. So if we are paying attention to the breath and using a phrase or mantra with the breath and also trying to feel in ourselves the meaning of the phrase, we are rather occupied. However we are busy with healing, calming and inspiring activity. That minimizes the thoughts. As we improve we can simplify our practice. To simply experience our being in the quiet of witnessing our breath is a great relief from our normal chatty state. However, it is also a doorway to much more - to encounter our Soul reality with all the peace and joy that that entails. Very rich stuff!

And down the road, when we have become more skilled, we may choose different types of meditation that suit our more advanced abilities and need. There are meditations used primarily for calming, for Soul alignment, for personal awareness and deeper insight as in mindfulness work, or for the building of divine loving energy in ourselves. Many combine all of those goals.

If at all possible, find a local meditation group and give that a try. A number of people sitting together working toward the same goal and bringing in fine energy can enhance our efforts and learning considerably. Find one that is right for you. Chapter 24 outlines the most outstanding and productive group meditation I have ever done and continue to do – Transmission Meditation. Group meditation is a very useful activity.

As I said several times any of Dr. Jon Kabat-Zinn's books on meditation are true gems. They teach us how to use any daily activity such as a rather mindless chore or eating or walking as a "mindfulness" meditation exercise. We are able to move to a state of peace in any moment of our day with some effort and practice. We need to learn to be in charge of our own mental state at all times and we definitely can do so. I use mindfulness focus for much of my day with great reward. Anytime I feel myself speeding up mentally or physically, I drop into the mindfulness breath and peace renews. It becomes more and more effortless.

Now for a few helpful hints that many have found useful. During meditation, sit with your head, neck, and back in a relatively straight posture, although not stiff. It is ill advised to cross your arms and legs unless you are sitting cross legged. Do not lie down to meditate unless you're ill or wishing to use it for sleep. A straight back chair is usually best and helps us to stay awake.

Don't eat any significant amount before meditation; the digestive process dulls our efforts and our experience. Allow three hours between large meals and meditation practice; two hours for smaller amounts. Of course a piece of fruit or something healthy and small anytime does not seem to be a problem. Sugar, caffeine, alcohol, and various medications and drugs, and a generally unhealthy diet can make good meditation much more difficult to produce. I was surprised at the improvement in my practice after a few weeks of becoming a vegetarian. That's not only physically healthy but spiritually healthy as well, but certainly not a requirement.

Begin by meditating fifteen or twenty minutes once or twice a day at about the same time if possible. If you wish, after several weeks or months, gradually lengthen your time to thirty minutes to see if it offers you even better results. Usually the longer our meditation period, the more quiet our mind becomes and the greater peace we feel. Do not abruptly stop a particular meditation period unless there is some emergency needing your attention. Giving yourself two or three minutes of gradual transition after meditation is very helpful physically and mentally. Sometimes you will feel sluggish or bored but stay with it. That's just another state of mind to detach from. Good things will definitely happen with your persistence.

It is also very possible that if you are feeling troubled in some way or have repressed difficult emotions and events, they may surface as you quiet yourself. For some of us our busy thoughts and activities are an unconscious attempt to avoid what is not healed. Actually, although uncomfortable, this can be very useful as it points us to the healing that is needed within. Many of the concepts we touched on in Part I may help you to bring greater peace to such inner pain. This would also indicate that considering MAP work would be wise.

For many of us some rather horrendous thoughts surface from time to time. As we go deeper, we face desires, memories, feelings, and urges that can upset us. They are present in us all. Part of spiritually awakening is being able to accept our personality flaws, wounds, and any unhealed material without judgment and remaining peaceful. It is usually our assessment of what arises that causes the discomfort even more than what is remembered. We've all got "stuff"; it's the human condition. Let's make less fanfare about it all. Chapter 23 is a magnificent testimony to staying the course even when old material surfaces calling for our attention.

Coping with distractions is central to becoming a successful meditator. All of us have many distractions arising such as our voluminous thoughts and feelings, body irritations like itching or aching, and environmental stimuli. The key is to simply notice when we are distracted and gently return to our meditation method. We will do this a thousand times over and become mentally stronger with every occasion which is not to say we can't scratch an itch or shift a position.

Make every effort not to chide yourself or feel guilty or inept due to distractions. That can ruin any meditation period. We all have plenty of distractions. I consider them one form of spiritual barbell and quite useful in a way. Just as physical exercise strengthens the body, releasing distractions strengthens the power of your mind. I find that metaphor very useful.

Some beginners use mental imagery to help with thought distractions. They imagine a gentle, gurgling stream in their mind's eye with little branches and leaves floating by. A thought pesters them and they imagine placing it on a leaf and watching it float away. Some folks place their thoughts in a bubble and allow them to fly on. Or make up your own distraction extractor. The possibilities are endless. Eventually we will need none of these things. Our focus and power of concentration will take care of what arises. That is likely to take awhile.

Many individuals I have joined with on the path have found that they have sequentially used several methods much to their advantage. Their first serious effort was to use a form of Mindfulness Meditation to become a clear witness to their own thoughts and feelings, becoming ever more insightful and detached. They gradually gave up their judgments of what they observed and felt immensely freed, not only during formal meditation but throughout their day.

They then went on to gain the ability to join with their Soul at the same time; to create that funnel of light through which Soul inspiration and intuition flows easily. Some have moved to an all encompassing meditation which serves the world as we serve our own healing. It has all come together for them in a divinely functioning way.

A little practical aside here: some meditators keep a pen and paper next to them. Terrific inspirations can come our way during our period of practice or maybe something important we have forgotten comes to mind. Without even opening our eyes, we can write a word of remembrance on the paper and get back to meditating.

Otherwise many meditations have turned to a new mantra: "I can't forget this; I can't forget this."

Most of us begin meditating for stress management, better health, a calmer state of mind, or perhaps a deeper spiritual connection. It is usually about some need or goal of our own. However don't forget others are very positively affected by our practice. Our state of mind is contagious whether we want it to be or not. One way we affect others is through our interactions which are definitely of better quality when we are calm. However, even without interacting, the energy we are emanating is healing and full of light through meditation.

Many take a few minutes at the end of meditation to send light and love to others or to the whole world in general. This is called radiatory service and is coming up in Chapter 25; it centers on radiating love and healing to those in need, serving our brothers and sisters. It's a wonderful activity. It is impossible to meditate and not benefit the world. No matter what methods we choose, meditation will produce positive results if we persist. Give it a good try! Do it for us all if you would please!! The world is in great need of your service.

Coming up in our next two chapters are fascinating and quite contrasting testimonies to what meditation and the paths they have chosen have come to mean to two of my dear friends. You have read in this chapter some of my experience which is more commonplace in many ways than what my friends will share with you in their work. I am grateful to them both for offering such vivid descriptions of their experiences on their journey home.

Chapter 22
Siddha Yoga: A Path to the Heart

by Carole Ann Al-Din, MSW

"God is in you and God is in everyone" are the seed words given to me by my Shree Guru, Swami Muktananda, which started the revolution in my life. Preceding my encounter with Baba (an affectionate term) dredging the dark night of the soul was a daily routine. For years I engaged in this daily pastime of bemoaning my life because my internal navigation system had seriously gone awry and malfunctioned.

In May 1979 while riding my Vesper scooter on a busy avenue in Washington, D.C., I spied a woman in a black van, gesticulating with her mouth. I became curious. So I called across the rows of traffic to ask her whether she was reciting poetry and she replied simply "no". I then asked whether she was reciting lines from a play and when she responded again with a resounding "no", I drove my bike over to inquire what exactly she was doing. Vasanti said "I'm chanting the song of my Guru."

This messenger was engaging in the repetition of the 183 verse song, *The Guru Gita*, which is chanted daily in the Siddha Yoga Ashrams and Centers around the world. Invisibly drawn by those sacred sounds and syllables, I felt the light of the Guru's consciousness stirring the strings of my own heart and setting me on the mystical journey that I walk today.

The word *Siddha* means "perfected being" which is the essential nature of each one of us. To experience this divinity within ourselves and within all creation is the mission and invitation of the Siddha Yoga path. The technology used by the Guru to awaken us to the divine power within is *Shaktipat*, a specialized and highly esoteric means of bestowing pure grace upon a student or seeker by a Master. This ancient initiation of awakening the spiritual energy, or *kundalini*, sleeping at the base of the spine in the *muladhara* or lowest chakra, is stirred through the Guru's word, touch, will or thought.

This sacred and secret transmission, which has occurred for centuries between Guru and disciple, has been given in unprecedented numbers to thousands of people without apparent preparation or discernible merit in the 20th and 21st centuries by Bhagawan Nityananda, Baba's Guru, by Baba and by his successor, Gurumayi, also known as Swami Chidvilasananda. It has been my great good fortune to witness the unfolding mysteries and revelations within others and myself under the direction and guidance of two living saints.

The enlightened state of a Siddha Guru is contagious. Yet, to fully embrace and embody the sublime teachings of the scriptures and become established in the unwavering vision and conviction that "God dwells within you as you", Siddha Yogis engage in *sadhana*, i.e. the spiritual practices of chanting, meditation, selfless service, and contemplation. To enter the heart, the divine splendor, meditation becomes our daily friend and companion.

Through the practices, particularly meditation, the evolution of my consciousness has grasped the understanding that *"the world is as we see it."* The dualistic mind forms an out-picturing or projection, which creates the heaven and hell in which we live. To transcend this dualistic and limited consciousness requires a paradigm shift. Through focused concentration and devotion to the inner Guru, the Self of all, we learn to make the pilgrimage to the heart, "the hub of all sacred places and go there and roam" as Bhagawan Nityananda commanded.

My journey thus far has yielded a myriad of delicious fruit: my external and internal dimensions have melded and thoughts and feelings aren't taken so seriously. My daily prayer "not to believe everything I think" is being answered. Contact with the Self, that part that is pure, blissful, universal, eternal, never tainted, untouched by doubt or any sense of unworthiness, is accessible as I take refuge in the Guru, live the teachings, remain focused on the goal, and have faith in the *sangham* or community of seekers.

Those blocks to becoming established in the awareness of the Self are evident as I commit to excavating, releasing, and transforming limiting beliefs. By practicing the virtues of friendliness, kindness, trust, patience (newly added to my repertoire), tolerance, courage, and equality of vision, the misery and suffering produced by fear and faulty dualistic vision are diminishing. Meditation unfailingly helps to calm the turmoil of the mind.

In learning to take small, steady, and scheduled steps, the goal of "attaining what has already been attained" as Baba once said, the God within my own heart is less daunting and the future is illuminated and bright. I offer my profound gratitude to you, Baba, Gurumayi, and Bhagawan Nityananda for the Siddha Yoga Path and for walking the path with me so that I know than I am never alone. I place my head and heart at your golden feet for the grace to fully unfold the *shakti* so that I may fulfill my divine destiny.

Chapter 23
An Experience with Zen Buddhist Meditation

This testimony to Zazen, a Zen Buddhist form of meditation, is very special. Few of us have the wisdom and courage to face the challenges, wounds and pain that we all carry with us to some extent. However, my friend, Michael, has this courage and for years has worked with his inner distress through consistent dedication to his meditation practice, knowing deep within himself that observing, allowing, and embracing all that we contain is a path to purer moments and, more ultimately and importantly, coming to release the belief that we are our experience as he so wisely shares.

Indeed, we are not our ego experiences. Facing the false realities that our egos have manufactured without resistance but rather with the witnessing that the meditative state offers us is, in my experience, a very royal road to awakening – a steeper and more direct climb to enlightenment. I deeply thank my friend for sharing this side of the awakening experience. Many consider it to be the "dark night of the Soul" and have found the statement "this too shall pass" to fortunately contain great truth. I have other friends who have practiced Zazen for years and each has had a different and distinctly personal experience of their meditation. We are all unique.

ZAZEN

by Michael A. Kirkpatrick, Ph.D
University Professor

The alarm clock, or my own fitfulness, calls me back to waking consciousness far too early in the morning. It is dark. The sun will not be up for an hour or more. I rise like an old man, my back hunched, my face grimacing, my movements in slow motion. I start the coffee in the kitchen, turn up the heat into the low 60s, and go back upstairs to the zafu, a small cushion on which I will sit for the next thirty minutes, or the next hour or two. I cannot say why. Despite the popular image of a Zen Buddhist monk in quiet repose, blissfully free of all human distractions and concerns, my experience on the cushion feels more closely akin to falling down a flight of concrete steps. My knees and back hurt, my mind careens through a virtual space of petty worries and anxieties, all the while terrorized by bogey-men of my own creation. Bad memories and tragic plot lines play out unbidden. I am a long way from peace.

When asked, I tell Zen teachers that my practice is "counting the breaths," Zen code meaning I'm a rank amateur whose attention wanders like an FM radio set on "search," jumping momentarily from one station to the next. Though speaking of a "goal" is anathema to Zen practice, my intention as a practitioner is to settle my attention on my breath, silently acknowledging its inflow and outflow with a counting cycle. With the in-breath I silently say "one," and with the out-breath "two." The next inhalation is "three," the exhalation "four." When I get to ten or drift off into reverie, I start again at "one" with the very next in-breath that I remember to count. That's it. Allow everything to be whatever it is, notice it, and return to the breath as many times as necessary.

My body and mind dance as I sit. Thoughts appear with their corresponding emotions, and patterns of tension grow throughout my form that leave me feeling like a tree that has grown twisting around a steel pole. I am turning, writhing within, as if possessed by spirits. There is a lot going on, none of which I want. My practice is simply to observe it, welcome it, and accept it. "It" includes my "not wanting." Sometimes the tension grows too great. I cry. I quit. I go off in search of coffee or ice cream or YouTube videos to distract me from all that which wells up within. I long for comfort that does not come. I feel the pain of the entire world. I weep over homelessness and hunger, violence and despair. More often and more selfishly, I shed tears over my own childhood feelings of abandonment and rejection. I continue to sit.

Over the twenty years during which this arduous practice has been part of my life, I have changed. From a youth who strived to be "tough" I have grown into a man who weeps to the harmonies of choral music. From a rational scientist I have grown to one who cannot stomach the animal research that once fueled my professional ambition. I have given up smoking and drinking and have learned to pray - a lot. My life practice and my meditation practice are two sides of a single coin. My attractions and revulsions contort and contain me, but the only way I know to be free of them is to allow them. I sit with whatever comes up, however lousy and offensive it is, however trite or nostalgic or momentarily joyful.

Zen Buddhism is, to me, an entry into the swollen and turbulent stream of reality. While there are quiet eddies and deep places of calm, still water, the overall flow takes me away beyond my own intention and desire. I have to let go and follow it wherever it leads. Doing so requires an allowing that leaves me terrified with insecurity. It is not something "I" control, though at the same time I vaguely recognize that I am the source, the fountain from which this river flows. I am beginning to release the belief that I am my experience. My identification with experience is softening, yet strangely bringing me closer to it. I sit with it, watch it, enter into it, and let it carry me away without paddling against it or attempting to hurry it.

Zazen is for me learning to swim in this river of earth reality, giving in to it and giving up for it. I make no claim about the rightness of this work. It is all I have. It is all I know to do. In a sense, it is all there is. It is not a "thing", a task, or an object within my experience. It is not like seeking God as a person with whom I can relate. It is reaching for the very ground of being, giving in to the source of everything, opening to a God who transcends my comprehension.

Chapter 24
Transmission Meditation: Advanced Spiritual Development and Service

s I mentioned in the meditation chapter, the most powerful and important meditation I have ever done is Transmission Meditation. I began that in the early eighties after spending several years on each of a series of other forms of meditation, all of which offered me growth and connection to my Soul. But when I happened on to this around 1980 or so, everything I read about it was so impressive that I had to see if I could get a group of folks together who might want to give it a try. And we did. And still do. In my opinion it is all it is stated to be. Many of us do it alone at home as well although that is of a slightly different format and potency and is described at the end of this chapter.

That is how I met the author of the major portion of this chapter. We experienced such a sense of this being the right meditation for us that we have stuck with it ever since we were group buddies in the eighties. Her name is Sheila Forester and she is my dear friend and sister on the path. The following few pages are an article she wrote and published on this important topic and I think you will find much value in it. Her article offers, as well, added information about our Masters of Wisdom touched upon earlier. Some of my own comments will follow.

TRANSMISSION MEDITATION BY SHEILA FORESTER, REGIONAL COORDINATOR, SHARE INTERNATIONAL, 2012

"Many of us would agree that a great spiritual transformation is taking place on our planet. Millions of people are awakening to the reality that we are not just our physical selves, and beginning to discover and nurture our divine, spiritual aspect. We are taking our spirituality into our own hands and seriously searching for ways to bring more love, peace and wisdom into our lives. We recognize that two great "royal roads" toward spiritual growth are meditation and service.

It is with joy that I share with you a form of meditation which brings these two activities – meditation and service – into one dynamic endeavor. That form of meditation is Transmission Meditation. It combines two great yogas: laya yoga, the yoga of service, and karma yoga, the yoga of the chakras. Either one is an effective agent in spiritual advancement; together they are incredibly powerful.

My involvement with Transmission Meditation began shortly after the birth of our first child. Laura was born ten weeks premature. Given her tiny size and complications, the doctors gave Laura only a 30% chance of surviving. Up to this point in my life, I had no interest in God and actually doubted His existence.

But with the frightening prospect of losing my baby, I did what any desperate mother with no faith would do. I began to pray. And it was through my crying out for help that I began to open myself spiritually. Once Laura was on the road to recovery, the Universe guided me to a group doing Transmission Meditation. Although I had no experience in meditating, the concept of working on myself spiritually as well as serving humanity resonated deep within me. That was many, many years ago, and Transmission Meditation continues to play an important role in my life.

You may wonder why we should engage in meditation at all. Certainly, meditation is a great tool to help reduce stress. However, the fundamental purpose of meditation is to make contact with our Soul, and to begin to bring our Soul's radiant influence into our personality. In truth, we are divine, eternal Souls in a process of gradually realizing our divinity through a long process of rebirth. The Soul on its own plane is perfect. But in its reflective state on the physical plane, the Soul is going through a process of gradual advancement.

We have indeed lived many lives, each one with the potential of bringing us more and more into the awareness of our true nature. As we draw closer to the end of our evolutionary process, our Soul brings us into some form of meditation. At first, we might give this spiritual practice just the slightest attention. Then there will come a life in which we make meditation a serious priority in our daily lives. Once sufficient contact is made with the Soul, we begin to desire to serve altruistically in some way. That is the major purpose of the Soul - to come into incarnation to serve the plan of evolution for our planet.

However, one of the problems facing people today is that we lead such busy lives, we often find little time left for service to any great extent. Many of us sense a readiness within ourselves. If only we could find a mode of service which would allow us time to accomplish it and also to care for our families, our jobs and live this modern life. Transmission Meditation has been the solution for many people. It is a dynamic form of service, yet can be easily incorporated into our schedules.

Through our spiritual quest, many soon discover that we have never been without Guidance. Particularly in this coming time humanity will begin to accept the existence of a group of enlightened ones, who since the beginning of time have watched over our planet and all living on it. For thousands of years in the Orient, the knowledge of these great beings has been commonplace. They have been called by many names: the Spiritual Hierarchy, The Great White Brotherhood, Our Elder Brothers, the Great Saints, and the Lords of Compassion to name a few. Students of esoteric philosophy referred to them as the Masters of Wisdom, our planet's spiritual hierarchy.

These great Masters are men and women who have gone before us on the evolutionary journey of consciousness. They no longer are governed by the laws of karma or rebirth and have perfected themselves. Many of these Masters make a conscious choice to remain on earth to guide and inspire humanity, as we too make our journey towards perfection. These loving Masters know the divine plan of evolution for earth, and are also custodians of great healing energies which are crucial for our evolution.

Transmission Meditation offers us the unique opportunity to work cooperatively with our spiritual hierarchy of Masters. The Masters are very advanced Beings. In their progressed state, They work with energies which are very high in vibration and are crucial to the healing of our planet. However, if simply sent into the world at that high rate of vibration, these energies, for the most part, would bounce off the bulk of humanity. Most of humanity does not yet have the spiritual sensitivity to take these energies in and work with them directly.

This is how service comes into play in our doing Transmission Meditation. Acting as intermediaries, members of the meditation group allow these high vibrational energies to pass through their chakras (the etheric energy centers of the body), which automatically steps them down into a more usable form for the average person in the world. The Masters then direct these "stepped-down" energies to where they are so desperately needed. A simple analogy of what transpires during Transmission Meditation would be using a transformer to convert 220 voltage into a 110 appliance. We are given to understand that it is beyond our comprehension to fully grasp the beauty of this manifestation. Suffice it to say, under the Masters loving supervision we are never in any danger doing this work, and actually benefit greatly.

The second aspect of Transmission Meditation provides the individual doing it with a great means for rapid spiritual growth. It is not possible to allow these powerful energies to flow through our bodies, our chakras, without becoming transformed ourselves. Many of us who do Transmission work have experimented with other forms of meditation. Although grateful for the enrichment other methods have brought into our lives, we wholeheartedly agree that Transmission Meditation has assisted our spiritual advancement far greater than any other meditation thus far.

According to Benjamin Creme, an English esotericist of some renown, who formed the first Transmission Meditation group in 1974, just one year of Transmission Meditation is equivalent in spiritual growth to fifteen to twenty years of personal meditation. It is truly that potent. And our lengthy involvement with Transmission has proven this seemingly outlandish statement to be so.

You may wonder how we go about bringing these divine energies into ourselves. To begin Transmission Meditation, we say aloud "The Great Invocation", a powerful invocation given to humanity in June of 1945. It was given to enable us to invoke the energies which would change our world for the better.

The technique required for this meditation is to bring and hold the focus up to the Ajna center, which is the 6th major etheric chakra located between the eyebrows. When we do this, a conduit is formed between our Soul and physical brain. And it is through this conduit that the Masters direct the energies. It is that simple. We sound "The Great Invocation", hold the focus at the Ajna center, and allow the energies to pass through us. We are asked not to direct these "stepped-down" energies ourselves. The Masters, in their enlightened state, have a much broader view of planetary need and know best where the energies are required.

Although the technique itself is simplistic, you may find holding focus at the Ajna center requires effort. We are given to understand that humanity, as a whole, is more emotionally polarized, which means generally our center of attention is lower than the Ajna center. Therefore it requires some effort and will to hold our attention higher. When our focus drops from the Ajna center, sounding inwardly the mantram "OM" automatically brings the attention back up. And the old adage "practice makes perfect" certainly rings true for Transmission Meditation. The more we do it, the easier we can hold focus for longer periods. We will also find the ability to hold a strong mental focus beneficial in other areas of our life as well.

Transmission Meditation is done by coming together physically in group form. This allows more energy to be safely transmitted through the same number of people than if they were transmitting alone. For example, the basic number of people required for a Transmission group is three – that is one triangle. The energy is triangulated, which potentizes it. Each person added to the group enhances the power of the group as a whole. If you have four people, you suddenly have four triangles. If you add one more person (a total of five), you now have ten triangles. With ten people, you suddenly have 120 triangles. And so on, in arithmetric progression. So the number of people in a Transmission group relates to the number of triangles, which determines the amount of energy the Masters can send through.

People experience the energies in various ways during Transmission Meditation. I personally know people who are powerful transmitters yet experience little during the transmission. This does not mean that they are less advanced than others, it could be the contrary. But there are individuals, who, because of their physical make up, are sensitive to vibration. One may experience tingling sensations between the eyebrows or in other areas of the head and neck. A few years ago a woman in our group could clairvoyantly see the energies as they passed through the group. Whether we experience anything or not, we are guaranteed that we are in the transmission as long as we have our focus centered at the Ajna chakra. We are guaranteed that we are serving the world well while advancing quickly spiritually.

There are some basic requirements of a Transmission group. First, members of the group must have a desire to serve; this will only be present if we have already made some connection with our Soul. Secondly, there must be a commitment to meeting regularly. The members of a group decide on a day, time and place and adhere to that schedule. The Masters then come to rely on that group to transmit energies at that time. Finally, Transmission Meditation is a serious process of conscious cooperation with the Masters. Therefore, members of a group are committed to service as their first priority and reserve any efforts of a personal nature during the meditation for another time.

There is no particular belief system required for Transmission Meditation, beyond the fact that there is a group of tremendously advanced beings overseeing our planet, who have our best interest at heart. Most people come into Transmission groups already possessing some form of spiritual or religious practice. They often find Transmission Meditation not only compatible but often enhancing other spiritual endeavors.

If we have no serious physical or mental ailments we can safely do Transmission Meditation. However, no child under the age of twelve should do this Meditation. Their chakras are not yet fully formed and they could be harmed. Otherwise, if you say "The Great Invocation", focus at the Ajna center and think OM, you can do Transmission Meditation.

This practice allows us to move away from a simple relationship with our own Soul to include a relationship with our Spiritual Hierarchy. Throughout the Universe there are beings who are transmitting their energies to lesser advanced beings, who transmit that energy down through those of even lesser advancement. Our Spiritual Hierarchy transmits energies to us; we in turn transmit those to all of the human kingdom, then to the animal kingdom, from there to the vegetable kingdom and to the mineral kingdom. Whether we are aware or not, we are working together for the evolution of all. As this energy exchange is continual, Transmission Meditation can be a mode of service that will last us for this lifetime and many more to come.

Since my involvement with this form of Meditation, I have certainly come a long way from that mother of no faith. Positive changes have developed quietly within me on all levels – physically, emotionally, mentally, and certainly spiritually. I find myself more willing to cooperate, share and work together toward the good of the whole. I have more understanding and greater awareness with more compassion and love for others.

For me, Transmission Meditation has contributed greatly to this positive development. And as a result of this growth, my attention has shifted from any personal gain I acquire from doing this work. I see clearly that Transmission is a privilege given to us by our beloved Masters to contribute to humanity in a unique, benevolent way. It is truly a gift from the "Gods".

And there ends Sheila's very informative and enticing article. What a marvelous job this is of sharing information on such an important spiritual practice. I am grateful. Sheila has several Transmission Groups in her home area, active for many years. And we continue to be blessed with one in our area. She has additionally co-founded many other groups through the years as have many others. These groups are found all over the world. More information on Transmission awaits you at www.transmissionmeditation.org/

Now a note on a form of transmission that does not require being in the same room with others. It is called Triangles Meditation and it was actually a precursor to Transmission Meditation. Many of us involved in Transmission do Triangles work daily. All it requires is that we mentally join with two other individuals who wish to do this service work with us as well. It can be done at any time of the day or night and certainly at any place. No coordination among the three people is necessary as to time or place.

After mentally connecting with the other two meditators, recite "The Great Invocation", preferably aloud if possible but silently if necessary. The triangle of three is important. And think and feel the meaning of these great words of prayer. The actual prayer is below.

This can be a very brief meditation wherein you simply go on about your day after forming the triangle and saying the prayer. Or it can be carried forward into a longer meditation allowing the energies to continue pouring through you. Many people combine this with their personal meditation or prayer time. In Transmission or Triangles work, you may or may not feel the energies and one who does is not necessarily more spiritually advanced than one who does not as Sheila mentioned. Its much more complicated as to who feels what than how evolved we are. It simply doesn't matter if we can feel what is definitely happening through us.

More information on this form of meditation is found through this website address: www.lucistrust.org/en/service_activities/triangles. And below is that very powerful and beautiful prayer used in both forms of meditation, "The Great Invocation". I shared this with you in Chapter 15 as well.

THE GREAT INVOCATION

From the point of Light within the Mind of God
Let Light stream forth into the minds of men.
Let Light descend on Earth.

From the point of Love within the Heart of God
Let Love stream forth into the hearts of men.
May Christ return to Earth.

From the centre where the Will of God is known
Let Purpose guide the little wills of men –
The Purpose which the Masters know and serve.

From the centre which we call the race of men
Let the Plan of Love and Light work out.
And may it seal the door where evil dwells.

Let Light and Love and Power
Restore the Plan on Earth.

Chapter 25
Radiatory Service:
Powerful and Practical

By the seventies, I had a few years of meditation behind me and was daily practicing exercises to further deepen my union with my Soul. This was steadily increasing the Light flowing into me and helping me to heal in various ways, body and mind, and gradually awaken to my true Self. It was just a beginning but a great gift to me. I was gradually becoming a better version of myself in all aspects of my life.

I'm reminded right now of something Neale Donald Walsch wrote in one of his first books. He helped us understand there is more to the Ten Commandments than most of us have recognized. He claimed they were not only an ethical value system to strive for but additionally a statement of what would naturally take place within us as we evolved. Our personalities would gradually conform further to our Soul's nature and our love would display in thoughts, feelings, and behaviors of ever more integrity and fullness. In the Bailey work that is called "Soul infusion". I've witnessed the truth of it through many decades of working with myself and others. As we achieve greater Soul union, we cannot help but become beings of greater wisdom and caring for all.

Our thoughts create our feelings and both contribute to the energy we carry with us and project unconsciously at all times to all around us as we have touched on before. We are, indeed, all contagious to one another. Energy rules! I enjoy making that point again and again. Unfortunately that applies equally to every negative thought and feeling we have and they too flow out and influence the world more than we imagine. So this is all the more reason to learn to control our mind with wisdom and deeper universal understanding of why and how things are. New perspectives create new thoughts and feelings and hence create new healing and loving energies for ourselves and others.

Somewhere in the early seventies I began reading the Alice Bailey material, that magnificent series of books which took a little adjusting to in vocabulary and flow. It is challenging, inspiring and empowering as you found in Chapter 8. One day I came upon the phrase "radiatory service" and how important it was to develop this within ourselves and how influential it could be in the world. I was hooked. And it was surely a "kissing cousin" to the group activity, Transmission Meditation, that I would be finding so powerful and yet more advanced a decade later. For me this was a precursor to Transmission and yet remains to this day as a companion to it in my daily practices.

The "radiatory service" theme emphasizes daily work of connecting with our Soul. That energy of Love and Light then naturally flows out of us and into the world. If we imagine ourselves, visualize ourselves, as this radiant sun with beams of Light flowing out further and further, it will intensify the effects.

A mantra that someone shared with me years ago that can be very useful in this meditative process was simply three statements repeated silently: *"I am the Soul, I am the Self, I am the Light Divine"*. This needs to be repeated with some focus and increasing belief and feeling to deepen that reality within ourselves. Quite a number of people have found these statements very uplifting and bringing about a deeper connection to their Soul, myself included. That is just one of hundreds of ways of calming and connecting, of meditating. You likely have some methods of your own. And when we use them, we are always sending wonderful healing and loving energy into our ailing world.

I must remind us all that this can be accomplished without our feeling any distinct energy in a physically observable way as we spoke of in the Transmission chapter. Some folks see wonderful lights and have visions of various sorts in meditation and otherwise – very encouraging yet distracting. I do not have those experiences. None of that is necessary for this service. I guarantee you that if you quiet yourself and focus on something spiritually uplifting and ask for Soul connection, things will be happening whether you can directly feel anything or not. Looking for the psychic sensations can be a serious trap and actually slow our progress.

I remember a story that went something like this: a young and eager meditation student ran to her teacher one morning excitedly exclaiming that she had just had a vision of a very great being during meditation. Her teacher very gently patted her on the shoulder and said "don't worry, my daughter; it will soon pass". I really love that story!

It makes the point that we can so easily get trapped in phenomena, anticipating each meditation or spiritual time of practice to be equal or better than the last, looking for more psychic experiences perhaps. This is a natural desire for us to have no doubt, but not productive. We are wise to cultivate a fresh and open mind without expectations for all the moments in our life, not just during spiritual practice. Now I am certainly not declaring all experiences in meditation are to be ignored. Absolutely there are times when very important understandings come our way through that medium. However that is more likely to happen if we do not have specific expectations and remain detached in our process.

I kept that in mind as I began to spend time doing radiatory service each day. I became calm and centered and reached deep within. I repeated my phrases with real feeling and asked for divine assistance in my efforts. Gradually I was able to extend this radiation to other moments in my day. That state of mind stays with us longer and comes back to us more easily as we continue our practice. Many of us simply drop back into this focus during activity multiple times each day.

As time has gone by, three words have formed a reminder that anchors me right into my radiatory service: permeating, protecting, and projecting. In accomplishing this service, several lines of work on ourselves and the world are accomplished simultaneously.

As we continuously strive to dwell in this state and the Light stabilizes further, we are indeed permeated within our entire being by this wondrous energy. And as long as we do not disturb that force with our negative thinking, it protects us from much negative energy that we might encounter in our daily routine. And it always projects out into the world offering a blessing to one and all. My three P's remain an important reminder. Radiatory Service is a blissful state in which to spend the day!

A primary factor in all this is that we need not leave our home to be a fine servant in the world. The contribution of loving energy is very important. No one need feel that they must be out and about to do any good. We are all invited to offer our best by just resting in our Soul space. And as we perfect this process, we find that we are this radiatory servant no matter what we are doing – serving in a soup kitchen or kicking back in our favorite chair at home. It is always all about the consciousness we are in at any given moment.

After several years of maintaining just this kind of focus whenever I meditated or remembered during the day, I was invited by my MAP Team to expand my efforts and availability for such service. The MAP chapter is finally coming up next. I was informed that there are a very specific dedicated and selfless group of beings, in and out of human form, who are working tirelessly to aid many people who are floundering in the demanding transitional energies of today's times.

I will just briefly say that this involves extended hours of meditative stillness during which I and many others are used by these great Servants to reconfigure and then transfer certain energies. These energies are then sent on to others in need in certain wisely combined streams. I do this most days of the week for many hours and some days I do better than others. However, although I am surely known to complain and whine at how my life has changed in challenging ways, my Soul urges me forward reminding me of the urgency of our times. Usually all I have to do to keep myself plugging along is to remember that some others are benefited by this work. So far that does it for me. I believe this was one of my "sacred contracts" pledged to before my birth.

Gordon Davidson mentions in his book *Joyful Evolution* a phenomenon that has been titled "helpers high". This is a reminder that the greater our service, in any pure form, the greater is the Soul energy that flows into us. This is a divine "high" that enhances every moment and aspect of our lives. We are amply rewarded for our efforts.

An image I have enjoyed is one used by the film maker Universal Studios. I imagine you've all seen it many times. It begins with the image of our globe and beams of Light begin pouring out from the globe over its entirety. I believe that is just what is gradually happening in our world. More and more magnificent and increasingly powerful beams of Light are developing and beginning to cover the earth. The Light is gradually increasing. I just love that image; it never fails to move me. I'm working on being part of one of those beams.

A particular prayer has continued to inspire me deeply for decades and I want to include it here. When we sit in radiatory service, our energy reaches out to others with many of the effects mentioned in this prayer. Many of you may know it and its inspiration and beauty.

Where there is hatred, let me sow love;
where there is injury, pardon;
where there is doubt, faith;
where there is darkness, light;
and where there is sadness, joy.
O Divine Master, grant that I may not
so much seek to be consoled

as to console;
to be understood as to understand;
to be loved as to love.
For it is in giving that we receive;
it is in pardoning that we are pardoned;
and it is in dying that we are born to eternal life.

From Saint Francis of Assisi

May we join with our Souls and rejoice in resonating ever more with the love and commitment contained in these words. I doubt that this prayer can be said with true desire without our becoming radiatory in that very moment.

Chapter 26
The Medical Assistance Program

A NEW AGE METHOD FOR HEALING

*I*n quite a few places in this book, I have mentioned MAPing and how valuable this process has been to me throughout almost twenty years. I never do a seminar without someone inquiring further about what this is and how they can learn about it. This chapter contains basic material on MAP so that you can assess for yourself its possible value to you.

In Alice Bailey's *Esoteric Psychology Volume II*, the Master DK sheds light on the ailments of disciples stating that certain emotional and physical ills are the likely result of our expansion of consciousness. In 1984, Machaelle Small Wright, founder of Perelandra - the Center for Co-creative Partnering with Nature and, in my opinion, the American version of Findhorn, was experiencing a reoccurrence of head pain which was caused by her ongoing spiritual expansion.

Previous to that time she had utilized chiropractic intervention to alleviate the discomfort; but this time Machaelle sought assistance from the Masters of Wisdom. They had become active in her nature research. These great Beings instructed her in a personal method of healing which joined her Higher Self, angels (often called devas), and other spiritual entities in an energy vortex which permitted healing intervention in all dimensions of her being – physical, emotional, mental, and spiritual.

Dr. Albert Schatz, Ph.D., discoverer of the medical breakthrough Streptomycin, has been most impressed with Machaelle's work and the MAP process of healing. He believes this to be a qualitatively different form of intervention in a heretofore unknown manner to take humanity to an unsuperceded level of well-being.

Dr. Schatz states in the forward of Machaelle's book on this topic, *MAP: The Co-Creative White Brotherhood Medical Assistance Program*, that this method actually goes far beyond offering us physical health. He believes it increases our understanding of our true identity and purpose in the cosmos, and our responsibilities and opportunities therein.

The involved members of the Spiritual Hierarchy have stated that this method has been given to us at this time due to our great need. It seems that much of humanity has outgrown its traditional medical support systems. Many of us can no longer make effective use of our contemporary healing interventions. MAP has been developed for our use to heal all aspects of our being until such time as the planetary medical systems can catch up to our state of evolutionary development.

The method is designed to effectively deal with what are titled "PEMS" issues. These letters refer to our physical, emotional, mental, and spiritual aspects as mentioned above, which are all quite interwoven in their causes and effects. Typical responses to learning of this unique method are "This is too good to be true and I surely don't merit such attention and care" or "Give me a break; this is too far out for me."

We are assured, however, that not only do we indeed deserve such an assist but, in fact, this isn't offered only for our personal well-being. The MAP Program is designed for the benefit of the entire planetary system in an inter-linking sense. In the difficult times in which we are immersed, the need for healed, well-functioning, spiritually committed individuals is great.

Through MAP we are gaining assistance in rising to the occasion of healing the woes of humanity and the planet. So not only are we gifted to have this method but have a responsibility to do our best to prepare for the demands falling upon all in these crucial times.

The MAP book lays out for us precise directions for utilizing this system in the privacy of our own homes. A problem list is devised by the individual who lays out the major "PEMS" difficulties requiring assistance. Quiet, private time must be set aside and the various members of the healing Team are invoked per instructions in the book. Our author asks that we read the information in the book for greater clarification and exact directions. A typical session itself takes far less than an hour to complete. It is recommended that a wise trial period for the process would be five months. As I say in seminars: "Any healing process I can do for free while lying down in my own home is definitely for me."

In the last two decades I have accumulated thousands of such MAP sessions. They are meditative and among the finest moments of my week as well as gradually producing impressive changes in all aspects of my functioning. I have become a more focused and dedicated meditator, many physical ailments have been eradicated or vastly improved, many old emotional blockages have been healed and released, and my belief systems and resulting thoughts are far more dominated by the light. What is accomplished is dictated by the problem list we give to our Team and the insight we demonstrate in developing it.

Most of this procession of events was gradual and gentle, some immediate and challenging, and many required a deeper awareness within. Certainly a willingness to relinquish my issues that have limited my progress has been required, very often easier said than done. It took me lifetimes to accumulate these problems so it takes patience and time to unravel the levels of what ails me.

I am indeed a better servant to the light as a result, as well as much more at peace, energetic, and one-pointed. Many members of the Transmission Meditation group with which I am affiliated are using this transformational method and have now increased their weekly meditative hours as a result of their enhanced dedication and durability. They are very pleased. This is likewise true of some of the members of our weekly spiritual study group; the results of their efforts are apparent in their interaction and understanding.

So the basic MAP system is used to work on any PEMS level of difficulty. Additionally, an assist is offered for any issue in which we feel we have some form of emotional or mental block or impasse. This is called the Calibration Process and is quite effective in its task of unsticking us when we feel blocked. For the person who has an understanding of the role that emotions and thoughts play in all of our physical and psychological ills, this is an invaluable resource.

The method is clearly laid out in the book in a most useable fashion. One can simply follow these simple directions. For those who seek a more intimate feedback system as part of their efforts, it is suggested that they work with direct communication with their MAP Healing Team. The Team has no difficulty hearing our communications; but for many of us hearing their response or advice is another matter.

The Spiritual Hierarchy members have suggested we develop our ability to "hear" through kinesiology. This is a method of assessing muscle strength or weakness and is used frequently in modern medicine. An affirmative response to our questions from Higher Intelligence strengthens us physically while a non-affirmative response brings about a noticeable, temporary weakness. Machaelle has simplified this into a two-hand testing procedure that is accomplished within seconds once the mind and question become clear.

Thus the healing may accelerate as we are able to "hear" their suggestions and follow through. My menopausal and allergy symptoms dramatically improved after I adhered to their dietary recommendations. Sometimes my sessions with my Team are shorter or longer or more frequent depending on their advice. When I had a sudden insight as to the emotional impediment preventing the healing of my leg injury briefly described in Chapter 6, their affirmation that I was proceeding properly kept me on track in my efforts. The two-way communication is invaluable. However, many people use MAP very effectively without utilizing this process.

Flower and garden essences - tinctures infused with the healing properties of various flowers, vegetables, and herbs - are recommended to accelerate the process but not required. These essences work directly with the central nervous and electrical systems of the physical body, as well as other aspects of ourselves, and can be used in both a preventative and remedial manner.

The Hierarchy Members working with MAP vastly increase the effectiveness of essences by specifying which are most useful to us at a given time and is another example of how the two-way communication can be a great benefit. At Perelandra, Machaelle has developed an excellent line of essences. I have been particularly drawn to the rose essences related primarily to spiritual expansion. I have MAPed both with and without these aids and was surprised at how much the essences accelerated the process and increased its ease for me.

The book also instructs us as to how the MAP process may be used with children. Again the instructions are clear and allow us to work with confidence. Likewise there are chapters which advise us in methodology for using a modified MAP with animals - domestic or wild. Here on our farm we have used this with success and gratification on many occasions with our own animals or a fallen bird or lame deer.

One of the most valuable offshoots of this process is the availability of Professional MAP Teams. After an individual has completed the basic five months in regular MAP sessions, accustoming themselves to the energies, processes, and opportunities, they are then eligible to initiate contact with appropriate members of the Spiritual Hierarchy to regularly seek guidance related to their professions, and many go off to work in connection with their Professional Team each day.

When I am linked to my Professional Team, I feel myself drawn up and focused in a higher state of consciousness, much more detached yet loving. I work as a psychologist as you know and as my Team works with me related to a given individual, I find that there is an element of wisdom and productivity in each contact that was not present before the Team's arrival. And, at this point, almost all my clients use MAP on their own and then the healing becomes impressive and surprising in many cases. Likewise in my teaching and writing, all flows more easily while being connected in this energy vortex with all Team members. The beneficial difference in my work is very tangible and rewarding. And how I love the company.

Back to the subject of kinesiology for a moment, even if someone is not attracted to the MAP process, to learn a method of communication with more advanced Beings is invaluable. Some people own the book just for that reason alone. The quality of life of MAPers' has truly improved by using the wisdom we are offered by our own Higher Selves and our Teams.

We live in times when the veil between seen and unseen worlds is being lifted. The Aquarian Age represents a joining of forces, a partnership among various handmaidens of God, be they angels, nature spirits, members of the Spiritual Hierarchy, Souls or humans. MAP represents one such form of joining with tremendous potential for the progression of us all.

The MAP book and other relevant materials, including one of my favorites of Machaelle's, *Behaving As If The God In All Life Mattered*, can be secured through contacting Perelandra at www.perelandra-ltd.com or by phone at 800-960-8806. All the folks working there are true gems and immensely helpful. Request a catalogue; the range of fascinating and beneficial materials is impressive, or just review them all on line. We can subscribe to their free email notifications which are terrific. Don't miss out on this! As I mentioned above, when I first experimented with this method I thought that any process I could do for free and lie down in my own room at the same time had to be worth giving a good try. Well, that was surely correct.

Following this chapter we have two testimonials from local experienced MAPers which will offer you some thoughts from others who seriously use this method of healing. I think you will enjoy them.

Chapter 27
Two Testimonials to the
Wonders of Mapping

The first is by Jill Saner, MSW

I have been practicing personal MAPing for two-and-one-half years and professional MAPing for about one year. I can say with certain truth that I do not know how I maintained sanity prior to this time. I am continually amazed by the miracles around me daily. As my life continues to become more active in all aspects, I am offered more and more love and help in managing it.

Prior to being offered MAP, I was in a place in my life where my relinquishing of traditional religious practice was necessary for me, but I was longing for a spiritual connection. I had a void and a great deal of guilt. I understood how healing it can be to participate in a church community and was appreciative of those who could receive in that environment. However, I felt alone and unreachable and that I did not belong.

MAP (Medical Assistance Program) is designed to meet the needs of and to support our human health. This includes so much more than what I thought of as medical. This care and support includes physical, emotional, mental and spiritual health (PEMS). When I began utilizing MAP, I was floundering with anxiety and depression. I was about to take on some of the biggest challenges of my life and could not focus. So I decided to look into this option which was presented by trusted friends - two of my precious guides.

It has been one of my greatest blessings. I have developed an incredibly beautiful and close relationship with both my personal and professional MAP Teams. I currently MAP with my personal Team about once per week and work with my professional Team almost daily on the job as well as in an academic setting. My sense is that my personal Team is with me most of the time and that there are many members who participate in both Teams alike. I have come to love and cherish them as they love and cherish me. I have never felt closer to a Supreme Being than I do through their devotion to and support of my growth. Our Higher Power gave them to me, or gave me to them more than likely, and I am so grateful! How blessed am I; I get to hang out with angels all day!

Lastly, other than the awesome gifts of spiritual growth and loving acceptance, I have been able to manage feelings of anxiety and depression, quit smoking and begin to deal with a host of other medical and emotional issues in the past two and one half years. I stopped eating meat about six months ago and have started to be very mindful of my diet and how this supports my overall health. None of this would have been possible without my Divine Helpers.

This is not to say that I still do not struggle with some remaining guilt and deficient self-esteem as well as many other issues that present themselves in the most interesting ways. But, today, I have a sense of hope and purpose that these issues are within my ability to address and correct with the abundance of help and love at my disposal. We always have assistance available to us at every moment. We are not alone. I hope that anyone who decides to try MAP has as an amazing and rewarding experience as I have had.

The second is by Eva M. Fisher, MSW

Writing about my experience with the Medical Assistance Program provides me with an opportunity to consider all the benefits I've received since I began MAPing. I started working with my personal Team a little over four years ago and my professional Team eighteen months ago. I've read others' stories of MAPing and I relate to many of their experiences as well. However, only within the past year have I begun to utilize my personal Team not only for physical health issues, but for help with my mental, emotional and spiritual growth as well.

One of the most important aspects of MAPing, in my opinion, is focusing on expressing myself well and increasing communication with my Team by asking questions that have proved important and helpful to me, as well as helping my Team to work with me more effectively. I continue to receive feedback and insight from others on their communication styles with their Teams. This insight applies not only to my forming more helpful questions, but also assists dialoguing with them about my reactions to their work. It is most important to provide our Teams with clear descriptions and understandings of what our requests and needs are as well as our comprehension of the dynamics occurring in our work together.

I've heard that many have close relationships with their Teams and even laugh and joke with them at times. I experience their connectedness and presence as well and feel unconditionally cared for and loved by them. I know they have only my best interests in mind. I once read a person's statement that they felt MAPing is a test of faith. It surely can begin that way, but my experience with them has taken me beyond that now.

I initially entered MAPing without feeling completely convinced, but in time I could see benefits and positive results of their efforts as well as my own. Several times answers have not come in the manner I expected. I think many people will agree that allowing ourselves to remove these expectations of what should or could be happening can be difficult, but the MAPing experience will teach us how to release those expectations. Only by recognizing answers and/or results arriving in unusual ways do many understand that letting go of expectations is important.

I am also pleased with the results of my professional Team. Once I developed a working relationship with them, my efforts as a clinician have become less stressful. I am better able to allow my Team to help me relax more deeply while in sessions. I recognize how powerless I am at times while working with others. After receiving education and experience in the mental health field, I relied only on my own developed and practiced skills. But since then I learned that I can receive and utilize effective help from above and deeper within myself. These combined efforts provide better results than I could provide depending only on my own effort and skill by far.

I feel that my Team is helping me to learn to get out of the way enough to utilize these skills with higher guidance. This can be hard to do at times and I continue to work on that ability. In many cases I am led to recognize the importance of being a better listener with love in my heart than attempting to inject my skillful efforts. However, I am still a relative newcomer in the field and recognize how much I learn every day.

With both personal and professional Teams I find it reassuring that I don't have to depend completely on myself, but can receive divine help. Both Teams are helping me to learn who I am and what I am capable of doing and what incredible opportunities are ahead for me if I am willing to be open to the experience. Thank you for allowing me to share. It has been a terrific journey and one that will continue through the years ahead.

Chapter 28
Blessed

By Deborah Sinclair
Brennan Healing Science Practitioner

*M*y life has been blessed. It has not always been easy, but it has been full of adventure and mystery. I have known from the "get go" that I am loved and supported by beings on higher dimensional planes of existence. I have lived knowing my life was unfolding according to a plan and even when I didn't understand what it could possibly be, I knew I wasn't alone.

I have always been able to sense the auric field, the energy that surrounds and interpenetrates the human body. As a child I spoke daily with spirits and angels. Although what my Mother called my "imaginary world" was always real and rewarding for me. For the first thirty years of my life my extra-sensory perceptions were also crazy-making. I was in grade school before I realized that the other children weren't seeing what I was seeing. By the time I was in high school I was filled with self doubt and battled depression. I never knew what to make of what I perceived, and for many years I felt unsafe sharing my perceptions with others.

Shortly after my daughter was born, my mother died. In the midst of funeral planning and the influx of family and casserole dishes from friends, I sneaked away from everyone to take a drive in the country. I wanted to be alone so I could have a good cry without bothering anyone or inviting comment. My mother had come to both my brother and me to say "goodbye" the night she died. We both heard her. He lived in Colorado at the time and I lived in NYC, but the distance between loved ones was no longer a factor as she shifted from this world to the next. We both knew she was at peace and content to be on her way, but on my drive that day I wanted some space to really feel my loss. Alone with my emotions for the first time since her passing, I let them flow in a burst that cracked the car's front window top to bottom, corner to corner. At that moment I realized that my energy field was more than something I could perceive. I realized it could have an effect. I stopped feeling "crazy" or "gifted" and began to look for real answers.

In the years that have followed that drive, I have lived a fantastic life filled with welcomed guidance and miracles. In 1996, the guidance led me to a Barbara Brennan School of Healing (BBSH) Introductory Workshop. Halfway through my very first experience as a healer that weekend, I felt a hard slap on my back. I looked behind me, startled, only to see the teachers quietly gliding through the room, guiding our hand positions with palpable love and support. I then realized it was my mother who had slapped me. It was her way of saying "That a girl! Do this!" It was a typical move on her part. Obviously a little thing like being out of body hadn't changed her a bit. I enrolled in the school the following fall.

BBSH is a four-year college dedicated to the Evolution of the Human Spirit. The school offers a bachelor's degree in healing science that is approved by the Florida State medical board, and licensed by the State's board of education. My experiences as a student there were demanding and extraordinary, beyond anything I could have imagined for my life. The teachers validated my perceptions and taught me how to context them. They supported me in reconciling early childhood and past-life issues. They helped me to develop my high-sense perceptions even further and taught me how to effectively work with energy to first heal myself, and then others. As I became more and more grounded, and expanded, in multi-dimensional awareness, I began to feel healthy and sane.

After completing the undergraduate program in 2000, I opened my professional practice that spring. I also went on to do three years of advanced studies at the school on the sophomore and freshman teaching teams and became certified to offer introductory workshops, like the one that changed the course of my life.

My intention as a professional healer is to engage my clients in the creation of abundant health. During a session my goal is to aid them in taking full responsibility for their healing process. From the Brennan perspective, energy and consciousness are interchangeable words. All disease, whether it is a psychological illness, cancer or a broken leg, is reflected in the auric field in a very specific way. As practitioners, we bring energetic awareness into the areas of the auric field and body that are blocked or distorted. When we are successful, our clients become more fully conscious of the ways in which they may have been distorting experiences in their life or blocking some experiences altogether, and their healing process accelerates.

Because the process is about enlightenment, a healing session with me may or may not involve lying on a healing table in a passive state to receive energy. Many times I choose to deliver energy through a process called harmonic induction, which is a conscious process of resonating in my auric field what is needed in my client's. As I perceive where the blocks or distortions are in my client, I bring awareness to those same areas in my own body as we talk. I also direct the conversation toward the psychological issues associated with the distortions within areas. I monitor the changes in their auric field as they begin to respond to both the frequencies I am holding, and the conversation we are having related to their issues. Often, long-held fears or memories being held in that space begin to emerge for deep discussion and reconciliation. Long forgotten feelings, ideas and images pop into their head and together we begin to identify the underlying issues that may have been unaddressed for years, perhaps even lifetimes.

I also do table work. A client will lie on my healing table as I charge their energy field, prepare them for surgery or reconnect broken lines of light along the meridians of their body. We learn well over thirty different healing techniques as Brennan Healing Science Practitioners, and I have used every one of them for a vast variety of psychological, spiritual and physical diseases in the past twelve years of practice. I have been privileged to witness profound transformation and healing in many of my clients.

I love what I do. More than anything, I am grateful for the sanity it brings me and the opportunities it presents me every day to validate, clarify or expand the experiences of others. In the chapter that follows one of my clients shares a brief summation of some of her experiences with me.

As I am writing this in March of 2012, it is becoming more and more apparent to many of us that our planet is in a period of transition. In conjunction with the Earth, people are waking up to multi-dimensional awareness and are having extraordinary experiences that many are finding themselves unable to context. I know this place. I know it can be frightening or confusing without illumination and guidance. I am blessed to have lived my life on the leading edge of this emerging wave as it leaves me in a position to ease others into an expanded view of the truly fantastic nature of our reality.

Chapter 29
Shared Thoughts from a
Brennan Practitioner Client

By Susan J. T. Hardman

*S*o many people have that aching feeling that something is missing from their lives, but I always had the overwhelming feeling that my life and all of life was overfilled to the brink. I felt that I just did not know how to access life well and how to tune into its energy. It seemed like there was some type of cosmic joke and I just did not get the punchline.

Then I was introduced to Deborah Sinclair, who has a remarkable talent to read the energy systems in my body and explain them to me in a way I can understand and tell me what is happening with a physical pain or emotional issue I am experiencing. After heeding her advice on changing my diet and lifestyle, I have been able to bring more consciousness to my spiritual life and make genuine progress.

I hold in sacred space the events of our sessions as Debi supports me in becoming personally engaged in my own healing process, many times bringing into light fantastic healing experiences that I know neither my imagination nor any hypnotic trance could produce.

Many of our sessions have dealt with my old issue of feeling I am just not good enough. I now see this feeling was based in fear that developed in early childhood and past life experiences. This has built up as scar tissue not only in my body but also in my mind and psyche. It was Debi's healing support that helped me face these fears by accessing those experiences so I could understand the insight they offered. This inferiority feeling was a defense I have developed to protect myself from feeling the overwhelming pain that my energetic and physical system was unable to handle at the time it occurred.

In one session I remembered myself as a very small baby. Suddenly, my sweet bliss of sleep was interrupted by two jealous siblings pinching me awake and telling me that I was not supposed to be in their family taking the attention and love away from them. I had no ability to cope with this at the time it occurred; but after experiencing it with feeling, sound and colorful sensations on Debi's healing table, I was able to work out that pain. It amazed me that I could feel the emotion and energy while making no judgment of my perpetrators or myself. I believe that is why I was able to let go of that scar and begin to heal it and to forgive the others who had added to it.

Debi has given me tools from an energetic perspective to work through issues like this one that I developed as an infant and elsewhere. I am now able to question the source of my belief systems and view my daily interactions with people more objectively. I am able to calm myself while looking at situations from a different perspective. Learning to view the world from an energetic view has allowed me to experience joy and peace in both my mundane and dramatic daily moments. It has also helped me see all of life in a more miraculous way.

Chapter 30
Seeking Divine Guidance

*Q*uite a few questions come my way on this topic. Those of us on the path become ever more interested in living the divine will and gradually becoming more attuned to knowing just what that is deep inside. However, for most of us there is quite a gap between wanting divine guidance and feeling assured that we know just what that consists of on any given issue. Here are a few thoughts on this and perhaps they may be of some use in your efforts. This chapter sheds further light on some of the concepts we examined in our "Heavenly Helpers" Chapter in Part I.

Seeking guidance is often prompted by our coming to know that we don't know what actions are most advisable and wise in many situations. Looking at circumstances through worldly eyes can, many times, be far from what spiritual truth might suggest. Acting wisely in any situation requires knowing many factors, most of which we do not have access to. So right off recognizing that we need divine guidance is a pretty good piece of wisdom.

No doubt such guidance comes to us automatically in many forms: a moment of Soul inspiration and intuition, through someone else's words, a coincidence occurring that we feel is not a coincidence at all, a song playing that really speaks to our heart, a dream, and so forth. Maybe we interpret most of that correctly; maybe not. Receiving authentic direction is very tricky stuff. Our ego desires can convince us we're on the right track when it is not necessarily so. My personal wishes have overwhelmed my listening ability many times.

This topic is also a very relevant one for me to again mention Gordon Davidson's book *Joyful Evolution*. An additional reason for seeking spiritual direction in a serious manner is that we are so often influenced by the contents of our subconscious mind. That can take us in counter-productive directions. Using the techniques described in Gordon's work can clear our path in a myriad of ways, all of which help us in receiving more authentic guidance. Unifying the goals and efforts of our subconscious, conscious, and superconscious minds greatly improves our effectiveness.

This is equally true of the MAPing process in Chapter 26. Being connected in that high vibrational dynamic allows us access to another advanced method for receiving accurate higher guidance. I have relied on this exquisite source of direction for two decades with ever-increasing benefit. However whatever approach we take, if done quietly and reflectively, the method becomes a meditation in and of itself. In addition to the instruction we may receive, the results of this practice of calm, detached, and one-pointed questioning and listening is worth the effort alone.

When I reach for that divine awareness that informs me of what is needed, I must take a few meditative minutes to prepare. I need to examine if my personal ego desire on that given issue is so paramount that

I have little chance of discovering the accurate path to take. Sometimes that involves digging rather deep. I've gotten in my own way many times through lack of sufficient insight into my own motivation and attachment to outcome. I ask my MAP Team to assist me with that deeper insight and they do. I want to see through my many layers of clinging and fear.

Again, whatever format for guidance we choose, this is the wisest inner preparation that is most likely to produce the finest result. Attaining the stillness to accurately examine our level of surrender is quite an art. I emphasize again that relinquishing our ego desires to that degree can be very difficult to do when the issue is something troublesome, urgent, or fear-producing. However, we persevere and improve.

Okay, so we know we don't know what's best at our conscious level and we've achieved some stillness and have given surrender and detachment our best; so what now? Well, lots of folks just state what they feel they need to know to their Higher Self or a trusted guide or MAP Team or a great Being we feel particularly connected to. It all ends up at the same source of higher knowing and ultimate reality.

Again I mention the MAP book due to its excellent instruction on forming a clear question. Without practice, we often offer up a question that is convoluted, contains mixed desires, and goes on and on. It is for our own benefit as well as theirs that we practice forming clearly and concisely in our minds what it is that we seek and phrase it with finely-tuned intention. The MAP book assisted me with that and it made quite a difference.

After making their best effort, many just continue with their meditation or their daily activities listening effortlessly for an answer. I mentioned the common adage that prayer is talking to God and meditation is listening. Productive listening is not a stressful effort. We simply continue working with our stillness and serenity and trust. Or perhaps we just go about our business relying on the fact that answers can come in a variety of ways.

Can all of us accomplish this on a regular basis initially? Probably not. Frustrations are common enough but we continue to forge ahead with increasingly good results. Our MAP author Machaelle Small Wright suggests that we practice with less consequential issues and observe our outcomes. Most folks working with this find that excellent advice.

When I am seeking greater wisdom on an issue in meditation, I do not expect to have any answer in my immediate awareness. Sometimes that takes place, especially when using the kinesiological method. However, I have found it very interesting that often my direction will not come into my consciousness until right at the moment it is needed for action. It is on a need-to-know basis in the sense of not knowing a minute before required. I believe that is often because there is great fluidity in our lives. We make new choices; circumstances shift and change due to many factors. The correct answer can often come to us only when we get right to the situation of concern. Perhaps occasionally a little test of faith is tossed in there for good measure—faith that we will be guided. It feels that way to me sometimes.

As I've shared before, a format for seeking direction that many of us use regularly is the kinesiology method as mentioned in our MAP chapter and described in detail in the excellent book. I've worked with several physicians and other health professionals who use kinesiology which is muscle strength testing for a variety of health issues. These progressive practitioners will test medications, foods, and functioning level of various body processes through these tests. However the MAP book teaches us how to get these yes/no answers using just our two hands. As I've said, some serious practice, both physical and mental, is recommended to become proficient in this methodology but once some amount of ability is gained, it is worth its weight in gold.

As I mentioned in our first paragraph, eventually we mature spiritually so that we live a life of surrender to our Divine Source; we dwell in a meditative consciousness as a matter of course. Then our knowing is surely effortless and well-connected. Meanwhile the practicing is excellent through other formats and assists us in arriving at the greater truth more quickly. Let's take seriously that our Higher Self is aware of a much larger picture than our personality/ego self and can guide us with much greater wisdom and facility.

Whatever method we might choose, it is the sincere openness that is important. We need to reach for that expanded vision on a regular basis and learn to rely on a source of knowing. Life will indeed go better as we gradually accomplish this. Some individuals say a sincere prayer each morning requesting that they be guided to God's will in all circumstances that day. They request help be given so that the lower self desires will not dominate. This is a great start to the day. "Not my will but Thine, O Lord" is a statement I cannot say too often. I know there is much repetition in this Chapter and I think it is all worth reiteration. I hope you find it to be so.

Chapter 31
The Art of Spiritual Cleansing

*I*t is not difficult to self-create or pick up negative energies. We have several energy bodies in addition to our physical body, all of which can attract unwanted energetic debris of many varieties. The energy bodies are sometimes called our aura. Our physical body has an etheric counterpart encompassing it and extending out a little further. It has often been said that any illness that reaches the physical body appears in the etheric body first.

We also have an emotional body that likewise encompasses the physical and etheric and then extends further as well. This houses our feelings and emotional reactions. Additionally, we have a mental body which encompasses all of these and extends and contains our thoughts and belief systems. There are many materials which discuss these in detail which are just an internet search away. The point is that we have more than just our physical self that can be tainted by negative energy or entities.

We will be immensely healthier and feel more alive if we regularly give our entire self a good energy bath. This facilitates our Soul connection and spiritual journey as well. Each of us can develop the ability to do this quite ably with a little practice. It is so worthy of every second we might give this effort.

Let's first touch upon what allows this negativity to develop which can produce a harvest of troublesome conditions within us. We'll start with ourselves. Life is not easy for many people in addition to the fact that the world has largely taught us to hold pessimistic, judging, and negative feelings generally. Thus, for us to have these darkened energies is very common. That means two things.

First, we have our own self-created darkness that weighs us down. Secondly, when we have our own negative thoughts and feelings, we are unconsciously inviting darker energies and entities to influence or attach themselves to us. The more pains and wounds we have within allow for easier contamination from the outside. That is part of the cosmic Law of Attraction. What's inside attracts what is outside, be it energies or a certain kind of person or situation. That doubles the trouble for us!

Even holding a belief in victimization is an invitation as well. If we are feeling victimized, which surely isn't unusual in this world, we are creating an opening for other people's dark energy to infiltrate our system. We've discussed in other chapters that there are no victims even though that strongly contradicts so much that we feel and see around us.

At the Soul level we have chosen our path knowing its opportunities for spiritual expansion. At our personality level, we make some unwise choices that create pain and havoc for ourselves and those, too, offer us the possibility of moving ahead spiritually if they are examined with reflection. Everything can be used to move us forward. Our belief systems and choices very much affect how vulnerable we are to the darkness in the world around us.

I never want to lose my compassion for all of life and the suffering it contains. However compassion is quite different than seeing ourselves or others as victims. We can love and support others without dropping into that space of thinking and feeling "poor them" or "poor me". That feeling opens another portal for wrongful energy to contact us.

On one level we are very aware of these energies and interchanges. We meet with one group of people and are uplifted and walk away with a lighter heart. We meet with another group and we are brought down. And we, as well, can be doing this to others. As said before energy is contagious.

I remember many years ago working with a beleaguered client who carried a tremendous burden of dark energy that we believed was connected to a misguided dark entity. We concluded a particular session and went our separate ways for the day.

I live a long way from my office and by the time I had arrived in the vicinity of home, I was observing totally despondent, suicidal thoughts in my own mind wherein I had been in a great mood previously all through the day. There was an energy within me prodding me to drive off the road into a steep ravine. I was very grateful that my years of experience in meditation allowed me to simply observe these changes in my mind without any identification with the thoughts.

I wonder how many people do some of the things they do through these kinds of influences, not knowing at all that their current feelings and desires are not truly their own. A few of my psychic friends have said they have been in prisons and psychiatric hospitals and seen many individuals there influenced by these dark energies and entities.

As soon as I arrived home, I stood in the shower (not necessary but helpful to me), called upon the Light of Christ, and immersed myself in that Divine Light and Love. It took quite awhile that evening to be completely cleared of that negative energy. I always ask that whatever the energy or entity may be, that it be carried to the very highest space of consciousness possible. That usually does take place. In more recent decades, I move through this process with my MAP Team which is very efficient in producing a fine outcome.

Had I dropped into fear, the energy would have been able to gain even greater ground. Fear is unnecessary, as unavoidable as it seems. There is no darkness that cannot be overcome by pure Divine Light and Love from above and there are many beings always available to assist us at these and many other times. It is easier said than done to develop this trust, I know; believe me, I know. However, we have excellent aid in doing so.

The next morning the client called me and said that he could not recall ever feeling as good as he had since our session the day before. He felt unburdened and uplifted as he had felt as a child. That was a great joy to me as well as him and a helpful confirmation to me as to what had taken place.

I do spiritually cleanse every morning and evening whether I feel a need or not. Developing spiritual cleansing into a regular practice will not only keep us brighter and purer but serves as well as further application in spiritual connection and focusing. This is a win-win to be sure. It is a gift to us but also a gift to everyone around us. Those close by are easily affected in many cases by our energy field. What an uplifting thing for them to have our clear energy around them. There is a huge cloud of dark astral energy that influences our planet that we humans have created through our emotional reactions throughout the millenniums. We do not want to add to or partake of that.

We need to recognize that we have power. We have the power to reach for and choose the finest of spiritual Light. Strong and clear visualization is a mighty tool. Imagine a force of great Light and Love flowing into every part of yourself. Feel the brilliance. Offer any remaining shred of fear, anger, guilt, or any negative energy to the Light and see in your mind it being cleansed away.

Do this with as much peace and trust as you can muster. We may rest in knowing that negative energy is not the Will of God. Feel the Light grow ever brighter in your every dimension. Stay in this visualization until you feel the Love and Light thoroughly and deeply penetrating you. Place your will and determination strongly behind this choice; this needs to be your intention and firm desire.

I have often asked for help in forming a brilliant bubble of Divine Light not only as a barrier to any incoming negativity but also used to prevent my own negativity from flowing out until I work it through. Here's an interesting tale of what happened using the bubble on one occasion. We have a little farm and one day I was working there on a task with another person. A little way into the chore, I began to feel rather resentful about it. I didn't want to do this. I observed this unwanted dark flow of thought and began working with it from my Soul perspective but it seemed to persist.

Since I was having some trouble dispelling this energy, I thought it would be best if I surrounded myself with the golden bubble so at least I wouldn't affect the other worker or pour it out into the world. I did so and about a minute later I began to notice that the thoughts weren't there any longer. I asked my MAP Team to clarify this for me and was told that the negative thoughts weren't mine but rather had been coming from the other person. I sent him loving thoughts and suggested we take a well-needed break from our efforts. Since then I've been much more careful in my investigation of what's going on when I experience something like this. This was a very instructional event for me. I use the bubble all the more now.

There is a terrific CD available through Perelandra (the Foundation that MAP comes from) that is a cleansing process. I believe it can be used personally, or for a room or house, or even for a land mass like our farm. The CD takes you right through very effective steps and is an excellent training tool as well.

Here are three additional suggestions. One is a visualization I was given by my MAP Team some years ago that I just love and find very powerful. I was shown the vision of a huge crystal bowl filled with water infused with radiant crystal energy. I imagine the bowl tipping over and the water running through every particle of my being or whatever I am cleansing. Of course this bowl always remains filled to the brim. I envision these radiant waters flickering with brilliant and energizing color and through their flow cleansing thoroughly. I keep my intention firmly on this process for whatever time is needed. It feels fantastic and I feel newborn after such a bath. Give it a try and see how it feels to you. In all of these methods, maintaining our firm intention to be cleared of darkness is mandatory. Our will must be firm. Again, we are powerful.

Gordon Davidson's book, *Joyful Evolution*, has an entire section (#11) on just this topic of cleansing ourselves of negativity. His suggestions go into greater depth and sophistication than I have here and I highly recommend it along with everything else the book contains. It is found at www.joyfulevolution.net.

Lastly, I recommend that those of you interested in working with these types of methods experiment and develop a process that really works for you. What fits well for one of us may not for another. Additionally, there are energy workers available in most areas who can be very helpful with these processes and offer good training. If this topic attracts you, look for a Brennan Healing Practitioner in your area to assist with this learning. We have much help offered from the seen and unseen worlds alike.

Chapter 32
Caring for Our More
Refined Selves

The potentially transforming energies being showered on our planet at this time can be very challenging and create a greater sensitivity in us. What once worked well in diet or physical habits or even thoughts may no longer serve us. We are in a time of dramatic change within ourselves and what our systems will tolerate or require for adaptation to the new energies has shifted.

In addition to this transcendent Light affecting us, practicing meditation for a lengthy period of time can bring about a much more impressionable and tender self which requires greater care and nurturance for our own comfort and health. Practicing yoga or other spiritual methods of development may well bring this sensitivity about as well. Many individuals are finding these times difficult in terms of nervousness, unusual aches and pains, mental changes and lethargy; many of us are just not feeling like ourselves and not understanding why. Some are reporting strange and sometimes recurring dreams. Our regular spiritual practices may feel different to us now and changes may take place. We're affected physically, emotionally, mentally and spiritually.

As a result of this we will delve into this chapter highlighting the immense value of caring for ourselves under these current circumstances. Even though we are not just our physical body, we utilize it in our learning, loving, and serving all through our time here. It is of immense importance. The habits of the world have steadily pushed us in the direction of poor care, especially in our eating habits. As we become more spiritually aware, our old routines will not serve. All the suggestions made here apply to the well-being of every aspect of ourselves. And we'll discuss much more than our diets.

When I began meditating, I was an impoverished graduate student and was eating very poorly. My cats were faring much better than myself. I was meditating for a few years before I felt called to work on my diet. As I slowly changed my intake of sugar, caffeine, white flour, alcohol and meat, I was truly shocked at how beneficially those changes affected my meditation practice. And that was in addition to the improvement in my physical stamina, health, and clear thinking. I was even a much nicer person to be around.

Making changes in a gradual manner when revising our diets is much more likely to lead to success than attempting to change everything at once. The huge sudden changes usually don't last long. They are too much of an adjustment to our system. I chose one particular habit a month to work on and that was a good pace for me. These changes took root, became habitual, and have lasted.

This largely took place in the 1960s. Now in 2012 we know so much more about our health risks and diminished capacities accompanying excessive use of the foods I mentioned. I remember a great Indian saint saying frequently that sugar is poison to our system. I really got lucky on that one; I'm the only person I know who is actually allergic to sugar. That has been so helpful to me in staying away from that substance. My will power needs all the support it can get. If everything we take in that actually injures us made us immediately ill, it would be a great benefit. Changes would come about quickly. However, alas, we must depend on our wisdom and willpower.

I'm not going to take time making a case against excessive use of each of those foodstuffs but I will say a few more words about meat. With a few brief relapses, I have been a vegetarian since 1969. I am not suggesting that everyone should do so. I have a lot of respect for Peter D'Adamo's book *Eating Right 4 Your Type* which advises specific dietary changes depending on our blood type. I do have the type recommending vegetarianism.

Even in the Bailey books, it is stated that not eating meat is only crucially important during the time frame preceding taking a spiritual initiation but doesn't place emphasis on it at other times. Listening to our own Soul intuition on this is very important. I think we all know that there are more folks turning to vegetarianism every day. What concerns me is that some of them are not on a truly healthy diet. To simply reduce or relinquish meat from our diets and not add the healthy foodstuffs can be risky. I eat deliciously and cheaply on whole grains, legumes, vegetables, fruits, nuts and seeds.

There is no death for any of us; we all simply pass on to our next destined dimension. Even vegetables and fruits have a life force that is cyclic. So for me death is not an issue. However, I have to say it still matters a great deal to me that every creature experiences the finest quality of life and peaceful death as possible. I'm probably preaching to the choir here in talking about supporting more humane treatment throughout the meat industry. However, that is another reason I stick to vegetarianism; I refuse to participate in that suffering. And I don't want to take in the medications and other substances commonly part of the life of an animal destined for our food supply. Fortunately, for those who can afford it, organic options are available today and many of those suppliers treat animals more humanely.

Likewise, most of us are more careful about our water these days and refrain from drinking harmful beverages. As we speak, a friend of mine is working hard to have the fluoride taken out of our local drinking water. This would be a fine service to all in the area. We have well water and filter it twice with very potent filters before using it. It is wise to examine the water you purchase closely. To filter our own water is quite important. I drink at least two quarts each day. Katadyn offers an array of excellent filters.

Here is another angle on how very important our food sources are. A very dear friend of mine is really up to speed on the importance of the enzymes we absorb from our food and how that affects our health. This is Deborah Sinclair, the Brennan Healing Practitioner who shared such fine material with us in Chapter 28. I'm going to add some of her words on this topic and a good reference in the following paragraphs.

The Enzyme Factor by Dr. Hiromi Shinya has had a great impact on how many view their diets and health. In his book he shows how to supply the body with the enzymes needed to trigger healing. These are found in raw foods, vegetables and sprouts. In his own practice he uses diet to cure heart disease, cancer and Crohn's disease, as well as autoimmune illnesses, fibroids and sleep apnea. He explains that enzymes are the key factors in supplying the energy that enables all of our bodily functions. When we deplete them, we get sick. When we replenish them, we get well.

Dr. Shinya knows that the body is designed to heal itself, and that our unwareness of this fact is making us ill. The book is well written and concise. It is an international best seller written by a true medical expert. Dr. Shinya's discovery of the body's own "miracle" enzyme could once again revolutionize health care in America. Glowing, vital health is within our grasp, once we understand the key to life's code-the enzyme factor.

Hippocrates Institute in Florida offers fine materials, supplements, and training courses related to all this information for those interested. Clearly this is well worth looking into; many have attested to the excellent benefits they have felt moving further into this mode of eating. When I have followed these guidelines, some wonderful changes took place not only in my physical body but in other aspects of my functioning as well.

So now we move on to exercise. Regular exercise from yoga and Tai Chi to walking and strength exercises are all very helpful. Hatha Yoga, Qigong, and Tai Chi are proven to be beneficial to our entire system. I was surprised how much more alert I was in meditation and life in general when I began exercising regularly, which I still do. Exercise becomes more important to aid us in staying balanced and grounded as we spiritually progress. And I doubt I need mention that maintaining physical cleanliness has an important role in our overall purity as well.

Here are a few valuable non-traditional health systems that we all can easily utilize and benefit from greatly.

These are additional implements for our more progressive tool box. Homeopathy is a form of natural medicine that very often offers spectacular results. My husband and I have relied on it a great deal for several decades; it is very inexpensive and has a long shelf life. We keep quite a varied supply on hand for everything from colds and flu to insect stings to arthritic and rheumatic aches and pains to headaches and on and on with no side effects whatsoever. I have a super one for exhaustion found at www.heelusa.com.

There are many excellent catalogues and books that explain the naturally healing principle in homeopathy. A very informative catalog in paper form and online is found at www.1800homeopathy.com or 800-466-3672. They have a splendid selection with excellent information and guidance.

As mentioned above, for years I have seen that the more an individual pursues spiritual disciplines, the more sensitive they become in what a human would consider both positive and negative ways. It is all to the good, however. We are more susceptible to the energies around us and more easily affected. We find great healing and support in more subtle forms of health assistance like homeopathy and the following alternatives. Don't be surprised if you react very differently to substances and environments than you once did.

It is commonly understood that students seriously on the Divine Path are very often fatigued. As mentioned, we are clearly more affected by other people, foods, and energies of many varieties, and we often are busy folks serving in the world in whatever way our Soul influences us to do so. For me, that's where that exhaustion remedy comes in very handy. The Bailey material calls us "the new group of world servers" and it can be challenging, demanding, and glorious work.

As a result of this sensitivity, many of us utilize various forms of flower essences. There is a great range of usage for these from common needs such as strengthening our immune system, reducing stress, increasing physical stamina, and rebalancing during depression to repairing higher vibrational Soul damage, releasing victimization and fear, stabilizing the body/Soul unit, and perceiving our Soul purpose. We touched on these in the MAP Chapter. I take them daily with great success. We are more subtle beings now and require more subtle health supports.

These essences are commonly found and studied online and in written materials. My favorite work is Machaelle Small Wright's book *Flower Essences*. I also order all of mine from her through Perelandra at www.perelandra-ltd.com. There are many good sources available. Consider doing yourself a favor and learn about these. These and many of the other suggestions are used as both a preventative and remedial intervention. Let's get pro-active.

And, as many of you know I'm sure, essential oils utilized as directed offer very helpful healing as well. There's a great deal of information around about those and they can be used in beneficial ways beyond the aromatherapy some of us are more familiar with. They too are relatively inexpensive with a long shelf life. I am never without a drawer of those close by. We get our essential oils along with our herbs from Mountain Rose Herbs at www.mountainroseherbs.com or 800–879–3337. Again, no one is encouraging me to mention certain companies. I just feel that when I bring up something that some of you may want to check into, it is appropriate that I offer you a starting place. I'm sure there are many companies out there with fine products. The internet gives us many choices.

The Bailey material states that there is no ailment that mankind suffers of any sort that does not have a corresponding healing substance found in nature. All of these types of alternative interventions can be used along with traditional medicine of course. But as we pursue our spiritual awakening, we often find we respond better to these more subtle forms of energy, since we ourselves have become more subtle forms of energy as mentioned. Many more evolved folks find they have increased difficulty utilizing traditional medications and interventions.

Let's not forget full-spectrum lighting that so many have found healing with emotional states that are reactive to limited sunlight, particularly in the winter. I use that lighting in several rooms just as a matter of course all year round. As human beings we are designed to respond to the natural rhythms of nature, but our lifestyles limit our exposure to balancing natural elements. Technology definitely lends us a hand.

Now some words about the power of the mineral kingdom. My spouse is a great proponent and user of stones of dozens of varieties. Many people find the individual potency of stones an important adjunct to their healing process and also daily maintenance of peace, calm, energy, courage, Soul contact, and so forth. I have studied this minimally.

However through the years, my husband has observed different needs I have had and chosen stones for me. I then verify with my MAP Team whether the stones would be beneficial and just how to use them–sometimes under my pillow, sometimes in front of my computer and television to ease the effects of the electromagnetic field, sometimes to carry in my pocket. I have been quite impressed with the beneficial effects. These are very subtle energies; often I can feel their effect right away and at other times it takes a while for their healing and supportive properties to have an impact. Either way they have been of great assistance to me.

It is likely that some of you enjoy the use of crystals and there are hundreds, if not thousands, of other stones with very potent effects as well. For those of us who are sensitive, these can be another very helpful tool. A good reference book for those of you who are interested is *The Book of Stones* by Robert Simmons and Naisha Ahsian ordered at www.heavenandearthjewelry.com or 800-942-9423.

Speaking of electromagnetic fields, many people (perhaps all) are negatively affected by the intensity of these fields around us. We are deluged in our own home. Bio Pro is one of many companies offering us products that greatly diminish the impact of these unhealthy energies. Before I secured these items, just sitting in front of my computer for any length of time was debilitating to some extent.

Somewhat related to this is material we discussed at the end of Chapter 20. There were a few paragraphs touting the healing and expanding benefits of current technology related to the uses of sound, light and visualization. That's a section well worth referring to again in terms of caring for ourselves.

An addition to that section is the book *Walk on Water* by Dr. Leonard Horowitz which is a scientific presentation of the power of sound and its application to healing and higher consciousness. This can be found at www.healthyworlddistributing.com or 888-508-4787.

There are so many new resources available to us today all related to healing ourselves and moving forward spiritually.

For the fiftieth time, I imagine, I again say please get a MAP book and consider strongly using that healing method or, if not that, practice the kinesiology method for questioning your higher consciousness and the Spiritual Hierarchy as to what you do need. We require expert advice as to which methods of wellness and healing are for us at any given time. We can all learn to access that advice for innumerable issues in our lives, certainly not just health interventions.

I believe there is a quote in the Christian Bible which offers us words from Jesus stating that what goes into our mouths is much less important than what comes out of it. The state of our mind and what issues forth from that consciousness is both a product of our health and a creator of it as well.

Thus, we must remember how curative and renewing love and Forgiveness are for us all. To feel these ever more powerfully, for ourselves and all creation, is a healing high beyond any I know. Again, now is the time, my friends. I will close with a challenging quote a friend sent to me from a source called "infinity-imagined" for our consideration.

"Stop watching television, stop watching movies, stop watching the news, stop spending hours on the internet, leave your cell phone and ipod behind. Every medium that claims to entertain and inform you is really there to pacify you, distract you, manipulate you, and enslave you. Free yourself, abandon the fake culture that captures millions in its illusions. Instead, fill your mind with the natural world, the intricate relationships and eternal cycles of the cosmos. Connect yourself to the universe in each moment, and you become something rare and beautiful, an arrangement of matter and energy that is the universe experiencing itself."

Well, that seems to be worth contemplating. It could be another huge step toward creating a healed, serene, and wise mind; all of these suggestions could be further steps toward living the life of our Soul.

Chapter 33
A Successful Day: Resting in the Joy of Our Soul

The essence of what I consider to be a successful day for myself has changed a great deal through the years. Although the shift has been and remains challenging, the end result so far has been terrific and I want to share some of the tale of that pilgrimage with you.

I revere that truth so often mentioned these days that "we are human beings, not human doings". Many of us are so busy, often by necessity; sometimes by choice. Many of us are evaluating our worth in terms of worldly defined accomplishments, often not even being fully aware of what our motivations actually are for our efforts. That surely has been true of me both in terms of not realizing some of my more hidden motivations and desires, but also in terms of allowing my self-esteem to rely too heavily on my worldly activities.

As we all know these worldly measurements are many and varied. Our self-esteem can rise and fall based on what others think of us, how much money we make, how well our children are doing, the quality and quantity of our possessions and toys, and on and on it does go. All of this is false identification. These things are not who we are ultimately. We don't consciously recall what our plan is for this life. We have no way of evaluating how "success" can rightfully be defined for ourselves or others. As difficult as it is, the quicker we free ourselves from dependency on what others think about us and the standards our society has laid forth for success, the happier and more peaceful we become. Our spiritual life can soar. We certainly become better role models.

I'm not saying there is anything wrong with having a comfortable life and things going well; not at all. Surely we care about our loved ones and want to do well at our daily activities. I'm challenging the idea that these outer circumstances should have any influence in evaluating our worth as a being or our estimation of anyone else's worth. And I'm additionally saying that to have those worldly kinds of goals attained may have little connection to our having had a successful day. We may have accomplished our plans while putting negative energy into the world and perhaps projecting stressful energies on a few or more individuals as we proceeded. It all depends on our inner motivations, desires and our state of consciousness as we move through the day.

Hence, we are greatly encouraged by the wisdom teachings to work toward knowing ourselves to be the Divine Eternal Self and identifying less with the physical body, personality and its attainments. This is the work of many lives. We are reminded repeatedly that our efforts would wisely be centered on our expanding consciousness rather than our usual exploits and circumstances. When we do so, often our worldly activities and involvements actually fare better. We often accomplish more in a day-peacefully, wisely and lovingly done.

Here's my story surrounding this issue. I had always been way too much of a doer and had allowed the success of my doings or lack thereof to excessively affect my feelings about myself. There was clearly an element of fear underneath many activities; I had to prove my worth, I couldn't disappoint others.

It was a few decades back that I was fortunate enough to have the luster connected to my worldly transactions and proficiency begin to fade. As I worked to identify and align further with my Soul, I went through a time of some disorientation. The old goal-oriented behavior in my days just didn't do it for me any longer. I continued to perform well but it didn't have the same meaning for me. At the time that left me feeling somewhat depressed but it was actually a very positive development.

Thus my old evaluation of things wasn't working any more yet I wasn't well grounded in a new and truer sense of worth. Ultimately, we will not be goal-oriented beings, but rather simply dwell in our pure being and allow whatever is needed to flow through us. This knowledge began to influence me in deeper ways.

Gradually during my period of disorientation, I began to define a good day in entirely different terms. I wasn't yet capable of surrendering myself completely to the activities of my Soul, but I did improve what I aimed for each day. I even used a worksheet for a while. I listed the activities and state of mind that really meant something to me and I would go through my list each day reminding myself of what behavior I now cherished and aimed for.

These activities of mind and body included being gently aware of my breath during most of the day's demands; this awareness gave me needed space for reflection. We can't beat the breath work! I frequently checked myself out for that peace of both body and mind sometimes using the "john meditation" we've discussed to hide away and give myself a few contemplative minutes. I was working toward slowing down my day in both behavior and mental busyness. I wanted clearer awareness in all things and to get out of the way of my Soul working through me in all matters.

As an aside, I'm interjecting a little humor here. However, this is a true image of the busyness of many of my days at that time. In addition to my private practice, I had the pleasure of being a college professor for thirty years. There were many maddening days of activity. I would sometimes hide in the restroom, since my office offered no respite, and relax to center myself for the next round. But try as I might, there would frequently be one or more students who would come hunting me down.

"Is that you in there, Dr. Jones? Those look like the shoes you wore today or was that yesterday? Could I talk to you about my term paper? Are you in there?" Really annoying I tell you. But it's a great example of the ego versus wise thinking. Of course my ego wanted to tell them what they could do with that term paper.

I remember the professor in the office next to mine had this little sign on his door saying "So many people and so few ways to tell them where to go". Not a commendable attitude at all I realize. However, I did allow a chuckle and could occasionally identify with the feeling. Anyway, at the same time my ego was complaining, I would take a few of those centering breaths and listen for the inner wisdom. Now in truth, anytime you have a student so dedicated to doing better work that they come hunting you down in the restroom, it's a great day for higher education and the student. My Soul would rush in with a saner perspective and I would respond within and without more helpfully.

Okay, so now back to my new loftier goals. The growing quietness of my mind naturally extended into that radiatory service I so treasure; I was able to extend patience and love appropriately and more frequently. That meant that sometimes I would just send loving energy out to others in need and that always lifted me up as well. Sometimes that love extended in behaviors that were more purely and wisely offered. I was particularly thrilled to have more moments of simply resting in the joy of my Soul. Peace cannot be over-rated, not in the feeling we have nor in its effects in our world.

When negative reactions of any kind arose, dropping into the breath for a minute allowed me to calmly release the emotion and, with greater astuteness, decide what, if any, action was required. I was asking for assistance from our "Heavenly Helpers" frequently. All of this was a gradual attainment and I still work on it each day, now with my Professional MAP Team at hand.

These newer aspirations added more valuable meaning to my life. Every day I would review how I had done with these more spiritually refined goals and examine how I could do better the next day. The luster lacking in regard to my worldly goals now gave way to a very fine shine on my new ones. I had much greater meaning in my life.

There is a difficulty with any work with goals and greater self-awareness. When we get in touch with not attaining our standards, it is very easy to fall into feelings of guilt and unworthiness. It is difficult for most people to separate taking responsibility for our behavior from carrying guilt, which is always self-defeating. That's why I found the teachings in our Forgiveness Chapter so valuable to my journey.

There were many days that I did not meet my hopes for my state of consciousness and its reflection into the world. I remember developing a little mantra-like phrase I used frequently when that happened to stay in a mental state of responsibility and change rather than lowered self-esteem and guilt. "Ain't nothing perfect about me" I would repeatedly chant, referring only to the personality self, of course. That true statement as defined by the world's perspective helped me to examine my lack through a more balanced set of expectations. Guilt produces fear and that slows down our progress.

Thus, as the lures and pleasures of this world continue to fade in attraction, I find that my current goals for my consciousness bring me joy and peace I have not known before. Someday I'll be beyond any personality goals at all and become a more pure vehicle for God's Will. The moments in which that takes place now are filled with bliss. But I'm taking it as it comes, one step at a time. I'm holding reasonable expectations and valuing improvement. Often I use another brief mantra with my breath which reflects our true Reality: "I am a perfect Child of God". You might say that a few times and feel what happens in your body and mind. I'm doing it right now. If you have belief in the truth of that statement, you will feel a higher and finer energy descend through you.

So you might ask yourself what you aim for each day. As you progress in your spiritual awakening, have your daily goals kept pace? Do you have any new vision of what you wish to bring to each day, each person, each situation and what you wish to bring to yourself? Spiritually nurturing ourselves daily is an activity of paramount importance. To take the time to evaluate our lives in this way can produce a much happier life and a more healed world.

However, just as I mentioned above that someday we will go beyond goals and live fully in the present moment and its Divine dictates, it is likewise true that someday we will go beyond our thoughts and belief systems. We will advance to a state of awareness that surpasses the activity of our lower mind and moves into the realm of pure Soul experience. Our transformation of consciousness will take us beyond the bounds of our present experience and into Divine Love and Light. All will be effortless and perfectly executed in our ongoing connection with God's plans.

Eckhart Tolle uses a phrase in his concluding chapter of *A New Earth* that makes my heart sing. He speaks of many of us as being "frequency holders". Some of us are here to simply ground the new transformational energies pouring in no matter what our outward appearance or status may seem to indicate. It is all about our level of consciousness.

I remind myself that *A Course in Miracles* asks us to reflect on its teaching that we are all destined to have a direct experience of God's Love. We are invited to enjoy all the transformation that Love brings. We are asked to remember that in actuality, often under the surface, we all love each other very much. That is surely part of the frequency that we are being asked to hold for the world.

And so we come to our conclusion of this book and, I hope, to your conclusion that your definition of a worthy day may be in the midst of change as well. Please remember: *Joy Awaits!* Make room in the stillness of your being for the inflow of the bliss of God. And please make room in your being for my gratitude to you for traveling this journey with me. I have very much appreciated your company. We end with a quote that my dear friend, Carole Ann of Chapter 24 fame, has sent to me. May it guide us home.

*The important thing is not to think
much, but to love much;
and so, do that which best stirs you to love.*

Saint Teresa of Avila

About the Author

Dorothy Jones, Ph.D. is a transpersonal psychologist, speaker, author and retired college professor. She has lectured on metaphysical belief systems and spiritual methods of awakening to the Higher Self for almost four decades. Her work as a psychotherapist includes practices for spiritual awakening as part of the path to healing all aspects of being. Dr. Jones lives with her husband of many years in the hills of West Virginia. Further information and spiritual thought can be found at www.JoyAwaits.com.

www.ingramcontent.com/pod-product-compliance
Lightning Source LLC
Chambersburg PA
CBHW030257290526
45785CB00001B/117